The 21st Century Predator
Resilience for a Burning World
By Cedar G. Elkheart

2

First Paperback Edition, September 2021
Second Paperback Edition, February 2022
Published in Moab, Utah
ISBN
979-8-9856615-0-7
LCCN
2022901286
Artwork by Cedar Elkheart
Cover design by Cedar Elkheart
Published January 2022 by Cedar Elkheart.

This storybook is dedicated to Ky and Crystal, two friends and Moab locals who were murdered in the La Sal mountain range in the summer of this book's writing. It is also dedicated to friend and fellow guide Alden Dennison, who died in the duty of stewardship to this land. These mountains and mesas now hold your hearts, as they perhaps always have. Trees have a way of remembering; you will be missed.

Preface
Mother Of All Bayous
Moab, Utah

"This is really why I made my daughters learn to garden—
so they would always have a mother to love them, long after
I am gone."
-Robin Wall Kimmerer, *Braiding Sweetgrass*

      I am a vegetarian. Much of my food comes from
something I like to call resource recovery. You may know
it by another term, like food rescue or, most fashionably,
dumpster diving. If it weren't for some of the things I find
diving, such as eggs, I'd be a complete vegan. My diet has
been this way for most of my adult life, and I find that it
brings excitement, challenge and nutrition to nearly every
meal compared to the highly processed diet I was raised on.
Diets that are not based on starch and carbohydrates are a
privilege of wealth--wealth of the land you live on or wealth
of the contents of your cart. It is imperative to recognize

this, but it was not always this way.

Six million years ago, someone somewhere on this planet stood up and became the first human being. Evidence indicates that we were eating meat long before this, and our modern food systems illustrate that most of us never stopped. Our lifestyles changed, our hunting and gathering was lost at the expense of free time and at the benefit of agriculture and homesteads.

In our present day, a short drive in any part of the rural United States will pull back the curtain and reveal the ugly truth behind the food systems that provide the calories for our offices, automobiles, and growing stomachs. I tell you all this because this book was supposed to be about coyotes. The clever creatures are so intertwined with this continent that it is hard to read any bit of history without a footnote about them popping up. Coyotes are amazing creatures that have learned to adapt and survive in so many different conditions that they are an exemplary model of how individuals can alter their behavior to survive. These canids are leaders that we should look to as we navigate the trials and tribulations of the modern climate emergency. They have proven time and time again that the fallacies and holes in our systems are identifiable and very, very real. All across the United States, complaints flood in about creatures of the night raiding trash cans. This is not an issue of these beings living in your neighborhood--whether they are bears, raccoons, coyotes or otherwise. It might be an issue that your neighborhood is in the middle of an ecosystem. It is definitely an issue of food waste. The animals wouldn't be in your trash if there was not something to be gained for them.

I am a vegetarian. To admit this is to admit that I have a definitive bias that favors living things. Some people like to give me a hard time about eating meat. To them, I say that I don't love animals; I just hate plants.

This book chronicles the story of one year of my life in Moab, Utah. I rent a cabin on US highway 128, also known as River Road. If I'm not in my cabin, I'm living out of my CR-V that I built out with white pine. Most rating systems, including my own, will tell you that this is the most beautiful road in the whole country. God's country, the old timers call it. The desert is a special place; this is recognized by most. The fallacy comes into play when folks come from out of town to try and force the desert experience on themselves, or worse, their children. This is not how it works, and it never was. This forcing of experience is not unique to the desert, but to all of our natural world. As human beings of this planet, we are all a part of nature, but to be immersed we must have a conversation and let the wind and the water flow between the two listeners. Most come out here and seek only to capture and not to listen. In this text, I also explore a great deal of the issues experienced from my perspective as a guide on this landscape.

I began this book to explore how we can learn from *C. latrans*, and how the beings can teach us about how to live lifestyles that are more resilient and sustainable. Since the first time I put ink on paper for this project, the climate emergency has been deemed officially critical. It is important now more than ever to look to our natural world for the solutions we need to build resilient, sustainable, and intentional communities. The coyote has proven over the last few million years that anything short of this will not survive. Some of the text in this book explores the canids from a scientific standpoint. When I first reached this topic, I knew that I had to acknowledge the inherent bias that I have toward the creatures. The feelings I have for them are big. I need to do something to negate this, or to equalize it. Utah's Predator Control Program offers a $50 bounty to hunters who kill a coyote and bring in its lower jaw and ears to the local DNR office.

Throughout the year that this book took place, I obtained a hunting license and took a 30 minute online course, and watched a two hour seminar about how to kill a coyote. The cherry stocked .308 rifle of mine belongs to the 21st century predator, and will kill the being by the same name. Equalize. Defeat the bias.

Some of the text in this book is vocabulary heavy and academic by nature, yet I want these stories and this information to be available to everyone. My beta readers (thank you, folks) have selected the words that are least common and we have made them available in a word bank with simple definitions. These stories bounce back and forth between a more research-based approach and a more emotion based approach to understand the complex interactions of coyote and human relationships; please feel free to skip a section if it starts to rattle your snake. The fact that these words are bouncing in your head right now and the fact that this text is in your hand means a great deal to me. I'm only here because of my love for this place, and I want to help others understand it as I hope to. Our landscapes can be fragile things, let's work together to protect them.

Additionally, an expansion of this text is available in podcast format, which includes interviews with Moab locals and outdoor professionals as we discuss many of the topics in this book. You can find it by searching the title of this book on podcast platforms.

The climate emergency on our doorstep is daunting. Terrifying. But not perplexing. The solutions are here. We have to be brave enough to implement them. The time has come and gone to wonder if we are doing damage, and to wonder how long we can keep this whole charade up. The time for community action is now. If you cannot find the motivation or the discipline to take action for yourself, do it for the next generation. This is a dangerous time where children look to us to lead in the face of peril. It is time to be transparent and teach them how to lead through tomorrow. The battle has already begun and we are just now realizing that the children are not to be protected and isolated, because they need to be in the arena with us. The coming decades determine the fate of humanity as a whole. No pressure.

Courage is contagious.
...
If you are not in the arena getting your ass kicked on occasion, I'm not interested in or open to your feedback.
-Brené Brown, *Dare to Lead*

Table of Contents

Dear reader,

Please make a note: while all stories in this text are as true as the squaw of a scrub jay, some liberties were taken to protect the identities of individuals involved. As such, nearly every name has been changed and certain details have been altered.

This is a small scale work and was done with the budget of an outdoor professional. That is to say, not much. It would be greatly appreciated if the reader could contact the author if they notice typos, blunders, mistakes, want to say howdy, have a moment of connection with the work, or have any cold soak recipes to share. The author can be reached at noceilingpath@gmail.com.

All definitions are provided by Merriam Webster, or myself
Word Bank:
Carbon footprint: The amount of greenhouse gases and specifically carbon dioxide emitted by something (such as a person's activities or a product's manufacture and transport) during a given period.
Greenhouse Effect: Warming of the surface and lower atmosphere of a planet (such as Earth or Venus) that is caused by conversion of solar radiation into heat in a process involving selective transmission of short wave solar radiation by the atmosphere, its absorption by the planet's surface, and reradiation as infrared which is absorbed and partly reradiated back to the surface by atmospheric gases.
Sequestration: To set apart.
Carbon Neutral: Having or resulting in no net addition of carbon dioxide to the atmosphere.
Pack Hunting: Hunting in a group by utilizing a strength in numbers and tactics that require more than a pair. An example is wolves surrounding or ambushing prey.
Monoecious: Having pistillate and staminate flowers on the

same plant, having male and female sex organs in the same individual.

Dioecious: Having staminate and pistillate flowers borne on different individuals, having male reproductive organs in one individual and female in another.

Relictual: As in, relic. Something that has remained unchanged from ancestors, even distantly related ones.

Search Image: A recollection of what a target should look like. An example of this is when a bear looks specifically for blackberries because it has had success finding and consuming them prior. It has developed a search image, in the same way you search for linguini in the grocery store aisle.

Habitat Fragmentation: The isolating of different habitats, usually by ecological destruction. An example is when a forest is divided into two by a new road.

Chaparral: An ecological community composed of shrubby plants adapted to dry summers and moist winters that occurs especially in southern California.

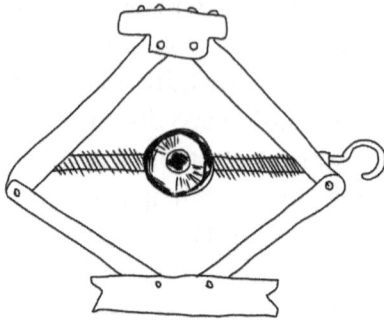

Belt Driven Machine

Belt Driven Machine

I take people on tours to make money.

I drive a Polaris Razor.

It is a belt driven machine.

It uses rubber tread to separate it from the rocks.

Its joints are lubricated.

It consumes fuel to propel forward, backward, and onward.

It is a belt driven machine.

It needs to be insured to be legal.

It should go in for maintenance check-ups often, but it doesn't.

It needs to rest after being worked.

It enjoys the trails.

It is a belt driven machine.

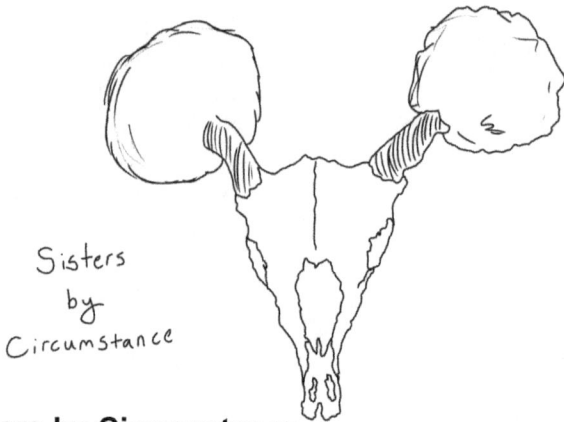

Sisters
by
Circumstance

Sisters by Circumstance

"There are just some kind of men who-who're so busy worrying about the next world they've never learned to live in this one, and you can look down the street and see the results."
☒ Harper Lee, To Kill a Mockingbird

We drove in a borrowed machine.

$60,000 worth of equipment granted us fuel, a sway bar and an LCD screen that displayed our

Pitch, yaw, and roll.

The ride was rough, but thanks to this screen we at least afforded the luxury of knowing what temperature the oil was.

It was rough, and far too long. Cabins left from the uranium boom, wind caves left from an updraft.

Graffiti chiseled into sandstone, he was here in 1907. JJ of the RMFTC (Rocky Mountain Fur Trading Company)

Comments between the two of us, Cam and I, about the
length of this trail. Accessible now to us in a full day's drive,
what would have taken horsemen half of a week or more.

Shorter to us, but it was rough. Rough, and far too long.

Headlights on, dusk.

Dampened blue and brilliant orange cascades in near form-
less whisps across the big sky,
A mackerel sky is what we call it. Altocumulus clouds undu-
lating like the bottom of the sea. Sometimes this can mean
rain. But usually not.

                                                        Then

I saw it,

but just barely. A charcoal black form lying in the darkness.
E-brake on.

We walked. A crater that could only be the result of two
hundred pounds of plastic explosives.

But I knew better.

I had seen him, two weeks ago on this same trail with his
water truck. Taking trip after trip to fill the ground and
make a pool of water for his cattle. A nod was all that was
exchanged.

Now, a caldera by fire of economy. Cattle need to drink,
after all.

the mud breathes.

I thought she was a calf at first, based on size alone. Most of her is buried in the earth, somewhere between a silty river bottom and quicksand. It pulls her down like the latter.

I lost a shoe and almost my whole leg to a mud pit when I was a boy. My sister pulled me out. This was like that.

I stick my fingers into her nostrils, pulling stone shaped blocks of soil to clear her airway. Totally horizontal. I slide one hand under the mud and rest it on her chin, lifting her other nostril from submergence.

Eyes up. Awake.

Her

lids struggle to open and a gastric sound escapes.

Exhausted.

"How long have you been here?"

Our eyes meet.

"Days."

She looks behind me, where another lies. Cam leaves lifeline duty for me. Cam is on it.

Steam emanates from the other black body, leading us to a fictitious conclusion.

A tear wells up and rolls out of her eye as I cradle her head. The drop weaves through the plates of cracked mud, a microchastic flash flood. Lizard skin.

Oh, Heif, is this how you died? In swallowed mud?

Sisters by circumstance,

Breathing together until one set of lungs filled with this caustic potion brewed by the cattleman?
 Until one of you stopped fighting and let it pull you into Opaque Lake

She answers with a moan when I put my forehead on hers.

I sink myself. It was not with all of my strength that I managed to lift her.

It was not with the help of her legs that gave out when she tried to stand with us that we managed to lift all 1,500 pounds of beef.

It was not with the juniper limb that we used as a lever to raise her from her tomb.

It was with nothing. And she knew that from the beginning.

We prop her head up with sandstone blocks.

"We're coming back for you," I say.

I want to lean in and make her smile. To make her understand. To ask her what you call it when a cow jumps over
barbed wire? To hear her laugh when I say 'udder destruction'.

And we do, five hours later. We drive 40mph down and back
up the moderately rated off road trail. 30mph faster than
any reasonable, non cattle-driven driver would drive.

There was talk of pulling her out with a tow strap and the
Jeep. But then she would not be strong enough to stand.

Humans bury one another.

At least,
At least this way she is halfway covered. Halfway interred.

At least this way we wouldn't break her bones.
At least this way it could be personal. And at least her finite
resolution would be known.

       To us.

       To the
Cattleman.

Selfish?

Headlights spill on the detonation site. A handful of calves look at us, then at the wounded and the dead. Orphans?

Soon to be, if not already.

I hold three rounds of ordinance in my jacket pocket. Cam holds much more than that in hers

We say hello and make ourselves much more than silhouettes. Her breathing is more labored. Sometimes it seems like she forgets to inhale for too long.

Her head slipped back into the mud while we were gone

While the last gasses of daylight burned off.

We get low onto her level, muddy again. Losing a boot here is just collateral. Cam is here to pull me out.

We clean her nose and her eye with water, pour some more into her mouth.

                              She does not drink.

                              The calves have
cleared out. Asked to leave the operating room with words unsaid. Don't ever let anybody tell you that cows can't speak.

The weapon of the 21st century predator is strapped to my back. The rounds, three of them, jingle in my breast pocket when I pet her.

She looks at us

"What are you doing?"

"This is for you, and only you".

And indeed it struck me that this was perhaps
The only time someone had ever looked at her
The way we did now.

Cam produces the pamphlet, written by poet and friend
Claire Wineman. Claire, upon hearing this story relayed,
would tell us that she knows it was written for this moment.

I stroke her gently and she blinks slowly. Knowingly.
I hope that we granted her mercy,
                                    And privilege.

Not many get to hear their own eulogy.

Cam whispers the softest whisper, a direct line from tongue
to spirit,

"to blow open"
*I imagined a bull burst apart on the road in one bodily
spot and*
The inside become the outside and
*The blood and other discarded functions looking as
precious as gold and rhodochrosite*
Spilling unceremoniously.
*Someone having hit this life which might have provid-
ed food*
*And probably wasting less than the meat-packing
plant may have,*
Because I can stand here and recycle his ghost
Matted glossy hide like maybe someone came to pat

him in the final hours, or maybe a sidebrush from a
fellow herd member,
Cattle morse code,
I-am-here-with-you-and-this-grass-is-so-damn-good.
Eye reflecting whatever he's seeing now as well as
the sky does the ocean
In a land-locked place
That warm and rusted ravine straight down the mid-
dle,
Like this road between the two fields where I came to
meet him,
The horns like worn teeth,
Dug in
But not survived.

And she blinks a Thank You.

The brass fits snugly into the receiver, a golden rocketship of deliverance, justice, and many other things.

7.62x51, .308, whatever.

We take a step back. I take a step forward.

One final ear scratch, a You're welcome.

I do not need to aim.

This bullet is guided by spirit & love & grace & mercy and she knows it when we lock eyes and I breathe and her sister does not and my finger moves four millimeters and the barrel of the rifle erupts in sparks and knocks the bats out of the sky and she contracts and struggles in the ground and is swallowed and the echo can be heard ten miles away.

And the sound is loud.
Her neurons fire
electricity in a symphony of neon spiderwebs
The muscles contract and fight in one final push to stand
And emerge from this death trap.

And I'm in the mud, bleeding and bleating. I'm trying to stand and I am scared and my eyes and nose are so dry and cracked. And although they are here, I am alone.

but she is not me. This bullet is not reciprocal.

A sharp inhale and the tension releases. The mud no longer clings,
but swallows.

I want it to be quiet, and I think Cam does, too.

Even when the echo stops, the spillway can be heard

Blood oozing and pouring down her forehead from that hole,
An uneven aperture of bone fragments.

It smells like copper. Like mud and blood.
And the sound is loud.

And her trip was rough. Rough, and far too short.

A Primer on Urban Coyote Populations
and
Patterns

A Primer on Urban Coyote Populations and Patterns

Introduction

Canis latrans, the coyote has long been the subject of mischief and misdemeanor in folktales dating from contemporary tales back to the stories of the original inhabitants of the Americas. With a relatively small endemic range, *C. latrans* manages both opportunity and challenges in order to occupy a position of tertiary consumption from the northern ranges of the sub-arctic to the arid sands of northern South America. The creatures are incredibly intelligent, sharing cognitive skills comparable to *Canis lupus* familiaris, the domestic dog. Fully mature and developed individuals exhibit both cognitive and social proficiency equivalent to that of a three year old human child. These proficiencies along with a variable physical disposition allow the coyote to thrive in radically diverse conditions. *C. latrans* has faced epidemics such as canine distemper, mange and tularemia, eradication attempts, and a vast collection of incidents and plights that have crippled other species. Still, the coyote not only survives---but thrives. Resilient and unrelenting, the coyote is truly a modern, 21st century predator.

Adaptation and Microevolution

Supreme adaptation ability is demonstrated by the coyote, and micro-evolutions have occurred on more than one occasion to aid *C. latrans* survivability. This adaptation ability is exemplified in Aducci et al. which concluded that coyotes in distant but similarly vegetated areas are more genetically alike to one another than they are to urban coyote populations. This morphological difference indicates that when introduced to stressors and variables associated with urban life, *C. latrans*' genetics are altered. In a 7 year study at the turn of the century, researchers at Ohio State University determined that urban coyotes have longer life spans than coyotes in their native range. Several traits and behaviors led to this longevity, namely the availability of easy prey such as rats and small domestic pets, readily available carrion in the form of roadkill, and avoiding humans by operating nocturnally. Indeed, several genetic and behavioral adaptations are observed as populations of coyotes extend their habitats to occupy different territories, which have not supported populations in the observable past. One remarkable trait is the practice of compensatory reproduction (not to be confused with reproductive compensation, which explains the survival of recessive genetic disorders), where *C. latrans* demonstrates the cognitive and physical prowess to birth 'extra' young in an effort to compensate for low survivorship of the prior birthing season. Using their adept sense of smell and hearing, coyotes are extremely effective at avoiding humans, choosing to become active at night in high traffic areas and avoiding social zones where human populations are more concentrated during this time.

Range and Competition

The great expansion of the coyote was seemingly parallel to the expansion of the American colonies on the east coast since the beginning of the Manifest Destiny era. The success of the creature in the aforementioned bioregions is attributed to one major factor: the absence of *Canis lupus*, the wolf.

As the onslaught of wagon trains and wool pushed onward through westward expansion, so too did the coyote in an ecological Blitzkrieg. These miners, prospectors, ranchers and pioneers went forth with rifle barrels hot as extermination campaigns began in an effort to level populations of *Canis lupus*. As wolf populations diminished across the continent, ecological niches were left vacant, but not for long. Within a few decades, wild wolves had been all but exterminated from the ranges that the modern coyote occupies. Primary accounts from this period conceptualize the idea that *C. latrans* does not have a preferred ecosystem, so long as food is readily available. This is one of the main contributing factors that led to the coyote being adept at adapting to almost any environment. Unfortunately, we lack detailed data on exact numbers during this era. It is unknown how far the natural range for coyotes reached, mostly due to the fact that humanity was not concerned with recording this data, and the fact that many different societies were contributing to stories of their own. Modern science had not been developed yet, so a comprehensive database of this knowledge is lacking.

What we do know is that this is the beginning of coyotes and humans sharing spaces. Unfortunately, in the modern world this often translates to the perception that coyotes are invading human spaces. A quick look at the history of any piece of land in North America will reveal that it had humans living on it for a short period of time in comparison to the age of the land. Is the deer crossing the road, or is the road crossing the forest?

Diet

The wild diet of *C. latrans* is entirely dependent on the region in which its population resides. The species occupies a massive range--from the northern tip of Alaska above the Brooks Range down to the northern reaches of Columbia. *C. latrans* find their homes in nearly every ecosystem in North America; forests, plains, deserts, temperate rainforests, chaparral, swampland and more.

The classical diet of the coyote is primarily comprised of meat, with a variety of insects and flora to achieve the necessary diversity for the remainder of the dietary needs of the species. In ancestral populations of coyotes, 90% of their diet consisted of the meat of mule deer, pronghorn, white-tailed deer, bighorn sheep, rabbits, snakes, lizards and larger ungulates such as moose, bison, and elk. *C. latrans* rarely attempts to kill larger prey, and optimizes meat consumption via carrion. At first glance, one may think that due to the fact that a large percentage of the coyote's diet is carrion, a symbiotic and commensalistic relationship may form with the wolf. A relationship such as that can be seen with *C. lupus*, the wolf, and other scavengers such as ravens, crows, and vultures. However, the relationship that occurs on the fringes of shared habitats is influenced more by competitive species interactions.

Competition

When *C. lupus* consumes their prey after a hunt, it is generally a communal activity involving most, if not all, of the pack. While coyotes are observed in packs, the majority of sightings are lone coyotes. Additionally, wolves practice gorging and rapid digestion, much like our friends in the felidae family, meaning that nearly nothing is left after a feast. After a carcass has been ravaged, little remains except hide and rumens, as well as bone. Wolves will continue to eat until no more consumable material remains, much like some domesticated dogs. This bulimic process is indicative that a vital part of their diet is missing (Bradshaw, 2006). When the amount of mouths to feed is factored in, as well as the fact that food is rarely left behind, it is easy to see how competition can form between the two species. To reproduce successfully, a wolf needs to consume 2555lbs/1160kg annually, and a coyote needs only to consume 550lbs/250kg. However, direct conflict over carrion or large prey will nearly always result in the success of the wolf. This does not come as a surprise when you consider that *C. lupus* can be two to three times larger than *C. latrans* when full grown. Who is more deserving of the meal?

Hunting Patterns

As coyotes expanded their range, ungulate populations grew, and a major factor keeping the ungulates in check is nearby populations of mid-size predators, such as the coyote and the wolf. These healthy populations of large ungulates grew, though not on as extreme a curve as they would have if coyotes had been absent.

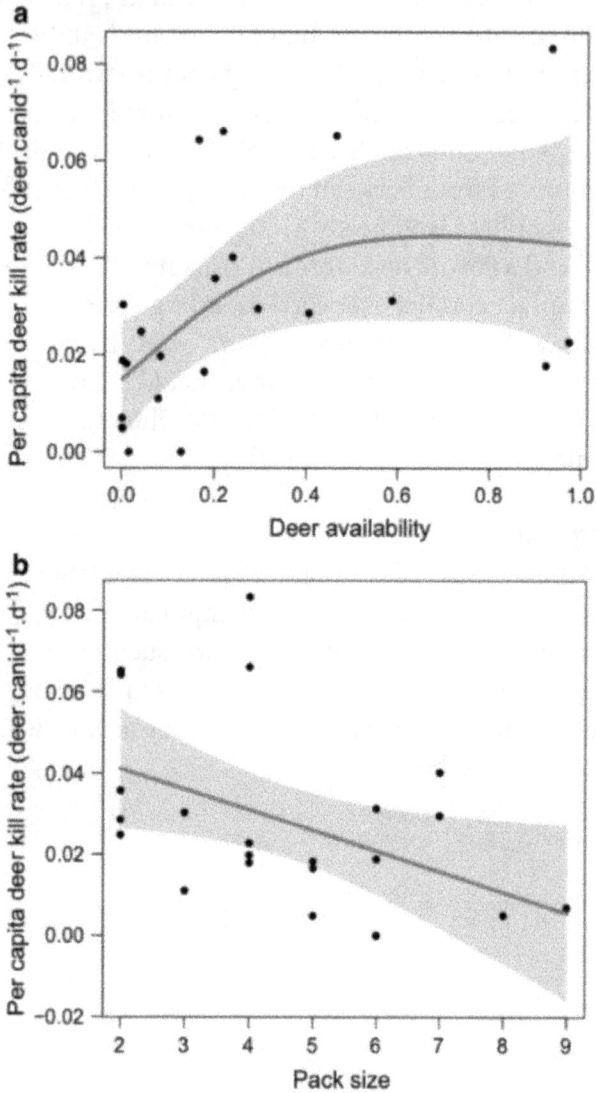

These charts from Benson's 2017 study indicate that there is a direct correlation between the decrease in coyote pack size and an increase in herd size of deer.

Although their biology classifies *C. latrans* as predators, t heir status as a tertiary predator is not as dominant as C.lupus. Notwithstanding, what they lack in hunting skill they make up for in creativity and ingenuity. Coyotes more than make up for their size on the hunting grounds by targeting individuals with significant disadvantages, such as starving or pregnant individuals, wounded and infirmed individuals, ungulates trapped in wintry conditions, and even stillbirths. All this is not to say that coyotes do not possess remarkable hunting skill. Packs have been observed to take down elk weighing upward of 400lbs/180kg.

Pack hunting here primarily involves groups of *C. latrans* surrounding weakened prey and using numbers to their advantage. The average coyote pack contains 6 adults in mating pairs, though only the alpha pair reproduces. Pups for each year are not factored in to this number. Changes in the physical distribution is associated with biotic distribution changes, requiring the coyote to expand their diet based on these changes. Fortunately, the ancestral diet of *C. latrans* trained pathways of hunting and scavenging that would be passed down somatically and instinctually from generation to generation. The diet of their forbears taught them what they needed to survive in these new lands. *C. latrans* finding nourishment from a scavenged bison carcass in the Dakota territory translates to the carrion provided by a caribou in Alaska. What once were kangaroo rats in the Utah territory are now shrews in the tropics of Columbia, where the den of a prairie dog was once overtaken is now the den of a fisher cat being cleared. This is a clear indication of a notably remarkable survival trait: a flexible search image. This trait exhibits intelligence beyond our typical understanding; the coyote not only understands the food they eat, but they understand how to apply their knowledge and experiences to new ecosystems to keep their stomachs full.

This ancestral diet prepared them for the food they would find in other ecosystems they would come to occupy.

The same diet comparison can not be made with modern humans. Then again, a coyote has never been caught intentionally tampering with the genome of a bison.

This significant change in diet and latitude brings up the question: Do coyotes in colder, more northern environments lack the gut bacteria to digest bacteria found in the late stages of rot, such as Erwinia chrysanthemi and Erwinia carotovora because cooler temperatures restrict the rate at which carcasses decompose? As global temperatures rise, will the microbiome of these northern coyotes begin to repopulate with digestive bacteria that once was vestigial, then gone altogether?

New territory often brought with it a great deal of failure as the new tenants had to learn how to be successful with fresh smells, fresh ranges, and fresh prey. This gap is often seen on a small scale as coyotes begin to populate new grounds, but does not significantly impact their survivorship curve in any way. Harrison observed in a study that some coyote pups left the den earlier than others. Those that left the den prior to 1.5 years of age can be considered transient coyotes and had an annual survival rate of 0.47. The resident coyotes, those that remained in the den for a longer period of time and perhaps indefinitely, had an annual survival rate of 0.74. We can therefore conclude that coyotes fit into the type II survivorship curve. This is potentially and most likely due to their extreme adaptability.

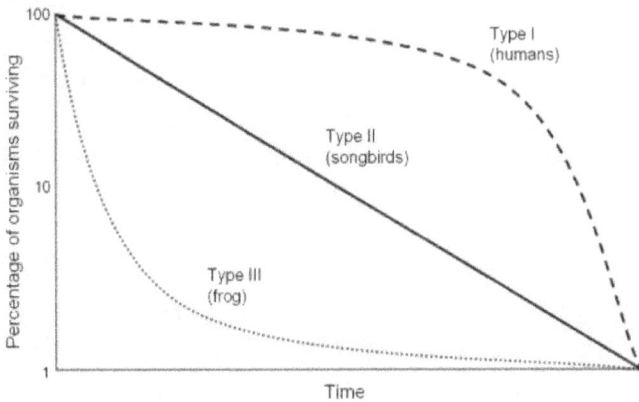

This generic survivorship curve made by Husthwaite for Wikipedia in 2009 illustrates the three main types of survivorships.

The fact that the survivorship curve was not impacted by territorial expansion is not unique to the coyote, but is extremely impressive. Such changes generally cripple most populations, as illustrated by contemporary habitat fragmentation as a causative factor for mass extinction. Of course, sacrifices still had to be made. This came in the form of an explicative diet. At their first hunt, pups often receive training in the arts of pouncing on grasshoppers. This training prepared them to incorporate insects into their daily diet, including caterpillars and beetles--two of the most common creatures to appear once the snow begins melting.

Additionally, the coyote began to consume a diet rich in rubus crops such as raspberries, blackberries, dewberries, and bramble fruit as well as stone fruits such as peaches and pears. Further, they will happily consume the melons, apples, and squash that you have been working so hard to grow this year. Contrary to the belief that all coy-

otes are on a keto diet, this adaptive menu is not restrictive
to fruit and meat--coyotes have been observed consuming
wheat, sorghum, corn, maize, and even digging up root vegetables. The manipulation and cultivation of antique crops
to modern equivalents by humans is an excellent example of
how the coyote benefits from contemporary society. However, it should be noted that this particular exploitation is
missing in urban coyote populations.

Things in this transition period are not always so
full of fructose, though. One supplementary caloric source
for coyotes is their own kind. The coyote has been observed
cannibalizing deceased conspecifics without hesitation. In
fact, effective coyote bait has been made in the past with
gristle from members of the same den. This indicates that
coyotes exhibit no observable preference other than preferring fresh meat to rotting meat. As the coyotes around here
tell me, "if it's dead, I'll be fed".

Competition and Predation Patterns

Competition and predation patterns have many parallels in
different environments that mimic the relationship between
the coyote and the wolf. In northern California, for example, grizzly bears have been the victims of extermination
campaigns in the past. Now, the ecological niche is exposed
and coyotes have begun to fulfill the empty role. Nature
abhors a vacuum.

Reproduction

The remarkable resilience of *C. latrans* is not lim-
ited to their ability to have a ductile diet and an ability to
spot open niches, however. Coyotes have found themselves
reproducing with several similar species. Although virtually
no populations have fully recovered from the devastation
caused by wolf extermination campaigns, refugees and survivors have always been present. Back east, we may observe

two distinct canids that are a testament to both the libido and strength of *Canis latrans*. The red wolf is likely a product of backcrossing, where the parents were a wolf and a coyote, then first generation offspring later reproduced with the parent or parent's sibling. This is a common practice in breeding and horticulture, but is seldom seen in nature except in extenuating circumstances, as described above. As wolves left their endemic territory, coyotes moved in and began mating with the remainder of the wolf populations. Over 70% of the genome of the contemporary red wolf is shared with the coyote. Can we call the modern red wolf a subspecies of *C. latrans*?

A 2010 study by Jonathan G. Way, Linda Rutledge, Tyler Wheeldon, and Bradley N. White focused on the genome of *C. latrans* in the Northeastern United States. The study determined that although there is great variability within coyote populations, they are not significantly influenced by

This factorial correspondence analysis illustrates eight microsatellite loci for five sample groups of *C. latrans*. The results of this analysis suggest that the mtDNA haplotypes in the two species that reside in Massachusetts are found in eastern coyotes as well as a new subspecies, Algonquin Park Eastern Wolves. This points to the fact that an increasing number of near conspecifics and potential subspecies have already been observed, but not through the lens of being related to *C. latrans*.

Morphometric Differentiation

The most simple comparison species to the western coyote is the eastern coyote. Though, both are thought to have developed new traits post-extermination campaign. Perhaps the largest difference between the two species is that eastern coyotes are larger, weighing in 21% heavier on average. Dentition is also a major difference, as tooth eruption occurs earlier in the eastern coyote. One possible explanation for these differences could be the availability of food. Eastern coyotes tend to inhabit habitats rich with resources, which could account for their larger size.

Cultural Influences

Prior to the Manifest Destiny period throughout the mid 17th century (1812-1867), coyotes could be found almost exclusively in two environments: the Great Plains region and the desert southwest. In Newspaper Rock Historic Monument inside Canyonlands National Park, rock images of *C. latrans* can be found in petroglyphs dated as far back as 2,000 years. In many indigenous cultures the coyote is a familiar face in stories, both good and bad. In one creation story, the coyote becomes impatient that the Black God was taking too long lighting each star on fire, and launched the remaining stars upward, creating what is now the Milky Way Band. In another, the coyote means danger. "If Coyote crosses your path, turn back and do not continue your journey." (Bulows, 2009)

This particular site is at a junction and has contributors from many cultures including Archaic, Fremont, Navajo, and Pueblo peoples. The name for this site in Navajo is "Tse' Hone'". In English, this means, 'rock that tells a story' (Markers and Monuments Database). Knowing that coyote human relationships date back so far helps to imagine why they are so ingrained into modern culture.

Urban and Suburban Ecosystem

The adaptability of *C. latrans* has been discussed, but what has not been discussed is the level to which the coyote is able to survive, and thrive, in urban environments that would typically annihilate other species. We know that sightings of urban coyotes have significantly increased in the last few decades, and we know that reports of incidents of contention have also increased. Consecutively and as a precursor, suburbia has expanded into territories that coyotes have already been displaced to. As a result, more and more wild canids walk city streets. We have observed micro-evolutions of sorts in coyote populations that have been displaced in the last 200 years. The most obvious of which is an adjustment to cryptic coloration. The coats of coyotes that inhabit the eastern states tend to be darker and more brown in color, while the coats of coyotes in the American west tend to be lighter and more sand like in coloration. The study is yet to exist, but it would be extremely beneficial to investigate the existing and potential micro-evolutions that occur in coyotes as we enter a new era where human populations and coyotes are struggling to coexist in a similar environment.

To further the effort, the study would also investigate points of contention. Main points of conflict include coyotes becoming roadkill, the slaughter of domestic pets and livestock, the exhumation of trash by the coyote, and other issues such as concerns of rabies as well as coyotes being mistaken for domesticated dogs.

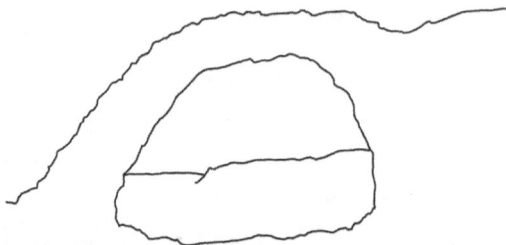

A Very Short And Incomplete Collection of Dumb Things Tourists Have Said To Me In Moab, Utah

A VERY SHORT AND INCOMPLETE COLLECTION OF DUMB THINGS TOURISTS HAVE SAID TO ME IN MOAB, UTAH

"Have the Yellowstone wolves made it this far?" At the trailhead for Grandstaff.

"So this is a...sand dune?" When looking at a plateau.

"So this is water?" The same guest, pointing at the Colorado River at 4,400 CFS.

"Is this underwater when it rains?" When pointing at Convent Mesa.

"Huh, I didn't think there'd be a gas station in Moab." A client from NYC.

"Does everyone carry a gun? Do you have a gun on you right now?" Upon seeing someone open carrying.

"Is this an arch?" When pointing at a cliff face.

"I love when these secret local trails are posted online"

Unironically referring to Left Hand.

"Where do you get your water if it never rains?" A client from Florida.

"Aw, I didn't realize I'd be getting so dirty. I'm going to have to throw these clothes out now" After receiving a light smattering of dust from the wind on white yoga pants.

"It isn't really like Utah is landlocked, because you've got the Salt Lake." A client from Texas.

"And all this erosion happens because sandstone is stronger than most rock, right?" At the entrance to the Devil's Garden.

"So this is the headwaters of the Onion River?" At Onion Creek Hideout.

"We didn't see anyone else on the road for an entire hour while coming here from Grand Junction. We wanted to turn around." Someone who has never left the city or driven at night, I guess.

"It's a shame that they just let the rocks fall like that, the government should really do something about that." Upon seeing a singular, softball sized rock fall onto the trail at Broken Arch.

"There aren't any guard rails!" At Green River Overlook. It is at this point that I tell them we are very natural selection focused here in Utah.

"Its alright to walk off trail if I'm just going to take one photo, right?" On Lathrop Trail.

"So if I clap, that'll make the arch fall?" In the Windows section of Arches NP.

"Has anyone ever run the full circle inverted through the arch? Like, skateboarded it?" At Sand Dune Arch.

Westwater

Westwater

Squashin,

You have not been around for very long, and I need you to know that you had a loving family.

Your death hurt us all, in our own way.

On the Utah-Colorado border lay Westwater Canyon. With Class V whitewater for some of the year, this is our go-to adrenaline spot.

The top of the canyon is composed of Wingate Sandstone, usually bright red and from the Triassic period, about 250 million years ago.

Below this is the ever-collapsing Chinle Formation, which is characterized by the green-yellow minerals.

Beneath this, in the roaring depths of the canyon, lay the Vishnu Schist. A jet black formation of rock that is only exposed due to an unconformity. The only place you can see this rock outside of the Grand Canyon. This rock is a part of the beginning, some of it could be 4.6 billion years old.

We run the course on a 12 foot raft, with me at the stern.

In the center of the raft is a cooler full of stolen ice and Westwater brand seltzers.

In it sits Monty, a tall, skinny, and muscular man. One of his favorite things to do is to find a problem, then find a product to solve it. Then, this man likes to give them as gifts. In a loving way, he always buys too many snacks to eat on his own and ends up sharing. He has a chronic addiction to Costco. He's lost his hearing in one ear, so I always try to sit on his good side. I think that is love.

Manuel sits on a thwart. He is here from Peru learning how to perfect his cooking skills. If you ask me, though, I'm not sure that they could get much better. Whenever he makes rice, he prefers not to use the refrigerator, but to leave it covered on the stovetop for days. It being the most delicious rice you could ask for, I often found myself asking if I could dip into this reservoir. The answer is always 'of course'. After the first time I requested to do this, an extra serving was always waiting for me. I know that to be love.

Beet Turnipseed stretches his lower back. Many names in this text are changed to protect the identity of their owner, but this is one of the few that is not. Beet's great grandfather arrived on Ellis Island from Scotland. Upon questioning, it was revealed to the onboarder that his great grandfather farmed beets and turnips back home. To 'Americanize' him, the onboarder renamed him Beet Root Turnipseed. This is who Beet is named after. We make eye contact and nod before a challenging rapid run. He is a farmer, leader, and spiritual mentor to me. We openly say that we love one another.

Cam sits closest to me. Nearly hip to hip, with just enough

room to swing a paddle. She smiles and looks fiercely at the whitecaps we barrel toward. We read the maps and make routing decisions together. She challenges those around her to be their best selves and to dare to lead as she does. This is challenging and frustrating work, but I know that this is love, too.

Mike Hawk sits at the front of the raft, smoking a cigarette. He usually wears camouflage and something entirely not camouflage in the same outfit. He thinks a lot, but likes to pretend that he doesn't. He throws in a few strokes of his own to angle his smoke downwind from me. He wouldn't admit to it, but I know that that is love as well.

You're rigged to flip with an NRS strap around the waist,a winter squash the size of a large human baby. They/them pronouns. Cam and I got you from the free bin at Moon-flower Community Co-op in June. I called to see when they would get another shipment, but the produce manager insisted that it was impossible that we got a winter squash from them in June. I would later return to Moonflower Co-op with a photo to confirm that you are a winter squash. The produce manager confirmed this identity, but again insisted that it was impossible. The birth of you is a mystery.

They say that the most painful thing about losing a loved one is that one may not have the chance to confess and repent. I suppose at this point I should tell you that you are adopted.

Sharpie outlines your chubby cheeks and a slightly mali-cious smile;we affectionately call you Squashin. Your social security card, however, notes your proper name: Dildo Baggins.

As a joke, I purchased a meat cleaver so small I could fit its entirety in my closed fist. I purchased this for 35 cents at Wabi-Sabi thrift store in Moab and promptly embedded it into the cranium of Dildo Baggins for a photo op.

This wound became gangrenous, or whatever the equivalent is for a squash. I kept you with me, watching as you slowly turned to compost and began to rot from that festering wound. One thing was clear. Our sweet Dildo Baggins did not have much time left on this Earth.

A month later, Mike, Beet, Manuel and I drove two hours away from the nearest paved road to an undisclosed location in the desert. We set you out in a field that had already been dozed from offroaders. We had taken Manuel shooting before, so he knew what he was doing. Mike's AR-15 loaded with hollow points waited patiently in the hands of the executioner. A character like Dildo could not go out silently. We stand, baking in the 115 degree heat about 50 meters away. Manuel aims at the rotting orange speck and pulls the trigger.

Dildo Baggins explodes into a cloud of sand and soil. Seeds rain from the sky.

Manuel exclaims and hollers in excitement.

He had no idea that Mike Hawk and I had mixed four pounds of powdered explosives (200-mesh zirconium hydride, 325-mesh ammonium nitrate, 600-mesh dark flake powdered aluminum, 325-mesh titanium sponge, and a few other things from Grandpa's Secret Recipe) and packed them inside. We had to give Manuel an American experience, after all.

But you know all this, my dear Squashin. I think perhaps

this letter was as much to you as it was to myself.

A weaker man (not myself) would say that the rot is what killed you.

My most impressive quality is that I am humble. You know this.

And so I will admit that it was not the rot...but the sting from my blade that led to your demise. I have learned from this mistake and, should your ancestor find their way to my table, they shall not only be spared---but revered.

Dildo Baggins, you are gone but never forgotten. Good-night, sweet prince.
Rest in Pieces.

All my love,
Cedar

Proposal of Research on Perceived and Actual Risk
of Populations of Canis latrans

Proposal of Research On Perceived and Actual Risk of Populations of *Canis latrans*

"I've been told by a few people, that when the apocalypse happens and all life ends, there'll be three things alive still. Cockroaches, coyotes, and Keith Richards of the Rolling Stones."
Walt Maldonaldo

Abstract

Canis latrans, the coyote, has been the subject of myth and murder for hundreds of years in the Americas. The preconceived notions that have been passed down through humans, both culturally and socially, perpetuates the idea that *C. latrans* poses a significant threat to many facets of human society today. This proposal identifies key points of contention that result in human-coyote conflict, such as roadkill, rabies, and the slaughter of domestic livestock and pets. A research study designed to collect data using wildlife surveys at 6 study sites is proposed to explore *C. latrans* adaptation and species interaction within those environments. This study proposes a "risk index" in which the surveys determine the difference between "perceived" risk versus "actual" risk to use by wildlife managers in urban/suburban environments to reduce human and coyote conflict. The study is designed to determine if *C. latrans* contributes significantly to these issues that existed before the expansion of their home range, or does some of the issue lie within the cultural, social, economic, and political components of human species interaction?

Introduction

C. latrans encroaching on human communities are perceived as an issue, but further data is needed to prove that they are, in fact, a problem. To measure this, additional studies such as Grinder and Krausmanm's Morbidity-mortality factors and survival of an urban coyote population in Arizona are needed. If it is determined that *C. latrans* is the key problematic species, the incitor of conflict, then how large of a problem are they? If they are not, then it would be beneficial to learn why they are perceived to be so. The main points of conflict between *C. latrans* and human societies are as follows: Roadkill, the slaughter of domesticated pets that include cats and dogs, the slaughter of livestock, the destruction of waste receptacles and the spreading of garbage, *C. latrans* breeding in urban centers, and spreading the rabies virus. These 6 issues each warrant an investigation of their own, and yet all these themes are all spokes in the wheel of our question: is *C. latrans* a problem?

Microevolution

Due to the fact that several microevolutions have caused significant behavioral changes in *C. latrans* over the previous two centuries, it is necessary to conduct site study and data collection for analysis in several different zones within the modern range of *C. latrans*. In an effort to clarify these zones for the reader, the potential sites for research are described below. These areas will be mapped and analyzed using a Geographic Information System (GIS). The amount of available area and range, perimeter, and landscape fragmentation will be explored as well as a geovisual analysis of wildlife corridors connected to urban/suburban environments for these sites. All statistics pertaining to human occupied areas outlined below have been aggregated from the United States Census. According to O'Leary, many qualifications must be met to determine whether or not a piece of research is accurate, even if it is relevant. By utilizing data from the United States Census Bureau we can meet many of these factors, including objectiveness, logical methodologies to reach the authentic truth, and consistency to name a few. The Census Bureau is under constant scrutiny and review, meaning that it provides peer reviewed data, a solid foundation for determining potential sites for this project.Based on the exploration of the peer-reviewed literature, landscape characteristics and land use were examined and used to identify potential sites that may yield useful data and results to help the author collect and analyze ecological data associated with *C. latrans* microevolution and adaptation to the changing landscape associated with human influence.

Study Site 1

Site One is located southwest of the Standing Rock Indian Reservation at latitude 45°35'10.9"N and longitude 102°46'04.2"W in Perkins County, South Dakota. This range is endemic for *C. latrans* dating back to the pre-contact era, the comically and scientifically named Bison bison, also known as the American Bison. The area is considered to be in the Great Plains bioregion, with little shade or large flora present. With a population of 2,897 people in the whole county as of 2019 in an area of 7,488 km², this location is an ideal research site to look into how a small, rural population interacts with *C. latrans* in its traditional range.

Study Site 2

Similar to Site One, Site Two also exists in the native range for *C. latrans*. However, it is significantly more populated and urban, as most of our secondary pairings of sites will be for this endeavor. Every set of two sites includes one urban and one rural site. Site Two is located in the Loma Del Rey District of Albuquerque, New Mexico. It is at latitude 35°07'50.4"N and longitude 106°33'03.7"W. A study that takes place here would have the opportunity to explore how *C. latrans* interacts with the nearby Arroyo del Oso Park as well as in an extremely urban environment. This area includes exemplary city planning, including green-scapes and a well thought out design that utilizes commu-nity and private space well. Loma del Rey is home to 57,108 people in just 45.93 km². Compared to Site One, which hosts 2.6 people per square kilometer, Site Two hosts 12.4 people, which is an increase of over 376%. The population disparity between these two sites is significant and under-scores the diversity of study areas, it may lend to wildly different results at the conclusion of the proposed studies.

Study Site 3

Site Three exists in the middle of the expansion range for *C. latrans*. *C. latrans* still inhabits these expansion zones, but it is not at the edges of their range. Site Three can be found at latitude 17°04'05.6"N and longitude 96°43'39.2"W in Oaxaca, Mexico. The city center has significant urban planning and works on a grid system, meaning that the city's future was predicted at a large scale well in advance. The surrounding area's lack of a grid system may indicate that they were developed without the help of a city plan-ning system, or ordinances. The area is considered urban, and is home to 300,050 people in an area of 85.48 km². This means that there are roughly 3510 people per square kilometer. One potential variable that may play a key role in the operations of *C. latrans* in the city is the presence of street dogs, which is generally not a consideration inside of the United States. Street dogs of the species C. familiaris may fill in some of the positions that *C. latrans* typically aims to exploit, such as exploitation of exposed trash. However, similar to how *C. latrans* is inferior in performance to *C. lupus*, these street dogs would likely not survive a direct encounter with *C. latrans* if competition was involved. Performance, in this context, refers to both physicality and mental capability. This involves variables such as advanced pack hunting tactics as well as larger, more powerful musculature.

Study Site 4

Site Four rests in the Yukon territory, southeast of Fairbanks, Alaska. Similar to Site Three, it exists in the expansion zone for *C. latrans*. It can be found at latitude 64°47'37.3"N and longitude 141°12'46.9"W. Adjacent to the Yukon River and near the town of Eagle, inside the site there is still potential for *C. latrans* to interact with human communities. Though, the town of Eagle is quite small. It has an area of only 2.28 square kilometers, data that the census represents in hectares rather than any other unit of measurement. As of 2019, only 86 people lived in Eagle. This means that there are only 37 people per square kilometer within the city limits. This is about 195% difference, about half of what we saw in the population density for Sites One and Two.

Study Site 5

The final two Sites rest at the furthest reaches of the current range of *C. latrans*. Site Five is in Winnipeg, Manitoba, Canada. It can be found at latitude 49°51'00.7"N and longitude 97°07'14.2"W, and is our more urban site. It has a population of 749,534 in an area of 464.1 km², meaning that about 1615 people inhabit every square km. At first glance, one might think that this is ideal territory for *C. latrans* due to the range being similar to their native range. However, this is not so, as they have not expanded beyond this site.

Study Site 6

Site Six, our final site, is at latitude 35°23'15.2"N and longitude 82°46'18.6"W in the Pisgah National Forest, in North Carolina. The prospective site rests near the Fryingpan Mountain firetower and Looking Glass Falls in Transylvania County. The county has a population of 34,385 people in an area of 986.8 square kilometers. The average kilometer contains 34.8 people. This exhibits a 191% difference between Site Five and Site Six. Notably, it contains a well used but still rural highway that may become a key research point when discussing roadkill.

Human and wildlife conflicts

Conflict Topic 1: Roadkill

For each of the topics discussed in this text, we will be aiming not only to discern realistic results, but perceptions as well. On the point of roadkill, how can we come to properly investigate the topic and determine whether or not *C. latrans* significantly increases the occurrence of roadkill? We can first isolate the determining factor to involve simply the advent, due to the fact that the 'danger' levels presumably increase as incidents increase. By exploring the conflicts in the human-coyote interactions, we hope to differentiate between actual risk factors versus perceived risk factors and identify patterns associated with these assumptions in risk. To obtain our data on roadkill, a mixed methodology of research is suggested. We need a form of qualitative research to determine the public's perception of such an issue. For the remainder of this study, assume that each human community listed above has a sample population that are objective and willing to participate in open research. To gather our data on perceptions, these sample populations of human individuals would be selected from each of our six Sites. They would be asked the following questions: is *C. latrans* a problem in relation to roadkill? Do you feel as though you hit or almost hit *C. latrans* when driving more often than other animals?

Aside from final data plotting and mapping, primary data would be collected by volunteer citizen scientists that are willing to participate in the project. When they hit an animal, registering it with the project would allow us to collect that data point. Being specific in other species that are common victims of roadkill would be useful to box in our data, however, our Sites vary so widely in ecological regions that other common roadkill victims would often be completely different species. Though, deer have such a wide distribution that 90% of reported roadkill incidents involve them. This statistic alone suggests that there may be a significant disparity between perceived and actual risk of *C. latrans* roadkill incidents. Results for this research would be most easily displayed for visual analysis in the form of a percentage based pie chart, with the results of the surveyed information presented in bulk percentages.

A quantitative approach to determine proportion of coyote individuals involved in vehicle strikes might offer insight into coyote hotspots within these communities. Further, we will determine conclusively if *C. latrans* is a problem in relation to roadkill. To determine the answer to this question, the study asks that the sampled population mentioned above records all incidents of roadkill for a period of one year, no matter how small the creatures are. Additionally, participants would be asked to write background information on the incident including weather, time of day, their vehicle, and their location. In doing so, we will accurately create a bar graph of incidents broken into categories that outline what creatures are hit and determine if *C. latrans* ranks higher than other creatures. Additionally, a plotted map is a useful way to present the results of this part of the study, and would provide insights on which areas are more likely to be hotspots for accidents. My personal prediction is that the most likely sites would be suburban settings within the historical range of *C. latrans*, as it likely has the highest concentration of the creatures and vehicles here are traveling at a high enough speed and are in a rural enough setting to instigate incidents of roadkill.

The roadkill species survey may encounter weakness in data collection and reporting. Not all incidents of roadkill are reported, which would significantly skew the data. There is a high chance that the human population would believe that reporting that they have hit something, whether it was their fault or not, would raise their insurance. According to the U.S. Department of Transportation Federal Highway Administration, 50% of large animal collisions involving automobiles go unreported. A further study in the future will investigate these logged, reported incidents in comparison to the logs of roadkill cleanup crews to build a more comprehensive picture.

Alternatively, we could see the opposite of this trend in data collection for animal strikes. In 1999, the state of Tennessee allowed those with a hunting license to legally collect, process, and consume animals they had killed on the road. This license encourages individuals who owned large vehicles to participate in a new form of pursuit: bumper hunting. Bumper hunting is the practice of intentionally accelerating or aiming your vehicle at wildlife in the road with the intention of wounding or killing it. If there is any reward for the survey, such as a coupon or a stipend, individuals participating may misunderstand and intentionally create incidents to be able to provide data, further skewing the results. More, the survey would not be comprehensive for the Site. Most people do not even know who their mayor is, or the news going on in their town. To ask them to report all incidents of roadkill and expect accurate results would be foolish. The results of this study will not be conclusive, but will establish a foundation for future studies. Furthermore, there is a significant possibility that a percentage of the sample group do not drive an automobile. We could always selectively choose individuals that do drive, but that would not be a fair representation of the population.

In addition, it has been proven repeatedly that untrained individuals often mistake *C. latrans* for *C. lupus* or C. familiaris, or vice versa. One additional prediction is that the percentage of roadkill incidents involving both street dogs and *C. latrans* will increase as the sample groups are observed closer to the equator. This is based off of personal perception of the concentration of visible street dogs throughout travels both inside and outside the United States and Mexico. Based on this theory, the reports of roadkill incidents involving canids would greatly increase at Site Three, in Oaxaca, Mexico. This project overlooks a massive geological region, including many transition zones, urban regions, and suburban regions. We must consider what the definition of these terms are. What defines suburbia? More locally, what is a desert? This is a question that I commonly ask my clients to get the gears turning. The most common answers that I receive are 'sand' and 'lack of water'. However, if we take even the lightest glance at meteorological data we can determine that the response about water is not true. Of course, a desert does not need sand to be considered a desert. Here in Moab, Utah, our annual precipitation is 9.45 inches, or 240.03mm. In the Wood Buffalo National Park of Canada, a boreal forest, they only receive 70mm more than here, at 310mm or 12.2 inches. In this national park, though, towering trees are abundant, and sand is not present. We must consider this when we reason that these terms are not black and white, but gray all over.

Conflict Topic 2: *C. latrans* and pet predation

Our second issue to address involves the killing of domestic pets by *C. latrans*. Violence and competition among canids is not uncommon, especially among wild populations. The assumptions that home-owners have of lawns is reflective of a physical boundary, whether one is there or not. Most lawns lack this sort of boundary, such as a fence or hedge. In lieu of this, many will establish a psychological boundary that strangers, including wild animals, should not cross. These boundaries, of course, are invisible to everyone but those that conceive them. However, a perceived issue begins to take shape when we consider that most individuals (particularly those subscribing to an HOA) consider their lawn to be a safe space, fenced in or not. Perhaps the idea of the modern lawn was introduced by Frederick Law Olmstead, who designed New York City's Central Park in the 1860s. It may come as a surprise to you that the park was fully architectured, designed, and constructed...not simply fenced in. This park created the idea that grassy areas should be landscaped, free of weeds, and should be aesthetically pleasing. However, in modern times that often translates to a 90 degreed box shape of uniformly cut, monocultured grass, usually buffalo or bahia grass (Bouteloua dactyloides & Paspalum notatum). There is an inordinate amount of content to unpack about lawns, but understand this: the idea of the perfect lawn was introduced in the 1950s, when conforming was expected. The first mass market homes were produced by the Levitts in the tri-state area, resulting in a strange concentration of towns named Levitown, Lev-ittown, and Leviton in the area. These homes were built for the purpose of housing veterans returning from the second world war, along with their new families. These soldiers had been trained to value neatness, right angles, and conformity. The result was the mass production and use of new gas powered lawnmowers to cut grass in the same way that the hair of most of these gentlemen were cut, as well as the production of highly toxic and effective 'weed killers'. These were the ancestors of modern day products such as Round Up (N-(phosphonomethyl)glycine, or glyphosate). To aid in this ideal, HOAs began publishing neighborhood newspapers with lawn tips on them and advertisements from the creators of these products.

It would not be long before endemic plants were all but stamped out, with the modern perception of them forever changed. To find an exemplary instance of how quickly and easily perceptions can be changed, we must look no further than the common dandelion (Taraxacum officinale) and the common clover (Trifolium repens). Both serve important ecosystem services, as all plants do. The clover digests atmospheric nitrogen and makes it available for use in the soil. The roots of a dandelion penetrate packed soil and help soil retention which reduces erosion, as well as act as an elevator of sorts for buried nutrients like calcium to reach the roots of shallower plants, like the clover. They also provide a system of aeration for the soil. This is far more than we could ask of any store-bought fertilizer. In addition to all this, both of these 'weeds' are completely edible, provided they haven't been sprayed with pesticides. I recall as a boy my parents would make fun of our neighbors, who were of eastern Asian descent, for harvesting the dandelions in their lawn and not mowing it as we did. According to Jo Robinson in Eating on the Wild Side, when "Compared to spinach, one of our present-day "superfoods", dandelion leaves have eight times more antioxidants, two times more calcium, three times more vitamin A, and five times more vitamin K and vitamin E." A new pesticide aimed at eliminating the atrocious yellow spots that dandelions bring to a perfectly emerald lawn, 2, D-4, was specially engineered at eliminating broadleaf weeds. As collateral, the common white clover died as well. This simple incident brought about a paradigm shift about clovers, which are now considered weeds. Lawns need to change and bring safe harbor to region specific crops that genuinely provide ecosystem services. Biodiversity is sexy.

All this is not only to promote polyculture and native pollinators (which is highly encouraged), but rather to call attention to how simple it is to change the way we perceive things. Although it generally leads to ruining the reputation of wild species, this phenomenon has the potential to shift the way that the common person views *C. latrans*. Perhaps they are not such a nuisance after all. The assumptions that home-owners have of lawns is reflective of a physical boundary, whether one is there or not. Most lawns lack this sort of boundary, such as a fence or hedge. In lieu of this, many will establish a psychological boundary that strangers, including wild animals, should not cross. These boundaries, of course, are invisible to everyone but those that conceive them.

Focusing on front and back lawns being considered 'safe spaces', most people do not realize that their pets could very easily leap over or tunnel under their fences. Such is the case going the opposite direction, too. Most *C. latrans* individuals possess the physicality required to summit even tall wooden fences. However, they lack the musculature that allows felids, such as mountain lions, to drag prey vertically.

Whether it is a rapier or wooden pickets, it seems like fencing is an effective solution to deterring *C. latrans* from harming your pets. Of course, there is always the issue of *C. latrans* not fully understanding the process of slaughtering a shih-tzu and then needing to drag it over the fence. And, the possibility that *C. latrans* will feed on-site remains.

For the perception section of this part of the study, it would be most useful to use a binary survey as part of the quantitative research. Due to the fact that the scope of this research is so wide, surveys are a good option because they are cost effective. This binary survey would simply ask citizens "is *C. latrans* a threat to your domestic pets?". One conceivable issue with this is that individuals may have animals they consider pets, but would not consider domestic. This could include stray dogs and cats that are being fed. Additionally, one stray animal could be being fed by multiple homes, skewing our data. Examined attributes would differentiation between indoor/outdoor versus outdoor only pets.

To determine whether or not *C. latrans* are a significant issue in the deaths of domestic animals, we would need to conduct a study for the length of twelve months. An additional study over the course of a 5 year period will explore the long-term trends of perception based off of this research model. These studies involve a comprehensive registry of pets, including their breed, weight, size, occupation and age to determine factors that may advertise these pets as prey. A citizen science survey collected for all six sites yields risk perception of coyote threat by ecoregion and population type.

My hypothesis is that working dogs such as shepherds and hounds that spend most of their time outside of the sterile environment of lawns are at a higher risk of being targeted by *C. latrans*, but not necessarily at a higher risk of obtaining mortal wounds. I originally predicted that the majority of domesticated dogs that fall prey to *C. latrans* are far from their ancestral roots of *Canis lupus*. Some of these breeds could include breeds of C. familiaris that have been bred to be deformed to exhibit flat faces, otherwise known as brachycephalic dogs. These breeds include both English and French bulldogs, pugs, most spaniels, shih tzus, boxers, and boston terriers. Although the selective breeding of flat faces causes a myriad of issues, including decreased respiratory response (and by proxy a decreased ability to flee) many other issues can be observed in dogs that have been "over-bred", in a similar way to how butter is served. The closer to their ancestral DNA these creatures can get, the likelier it is that they would be able to hold their ground against *C. latrans.*

This graph designed by Parker et al. illustrates the relationship of dog breeds to one another. The ancestral breeds most closely related to *C. lupus*, the wolf, can be seen at the 3 o'clock heading in black. Conversely, more distantly related conspecifics can be seen as we travel further around the sphere. Based on this, we can see that the 7 breeds of dog most closely related to the wolf are Basenjis, Xigous, Chinese and American breeds of Tibetan Mastiffs, Siberian Huskys, Greenland Sledge Dogs, and Alaskan Malamutes. My initial hypothesis was that the more steps taken toward the exterior of the circle, the more likely the creature could become the victim of a *C. latrans* attack if the scenario was consistent. For example, an English Springer Spaniel may be less likely to be a victim than the English Cocker Spaniel, because the Cocker Spaniel falls further away from the original ancestor. However, this clearly cannot be the case. If it were, it would mean that a chihuahua is more physically adept at fighting off a predator than an American Staffordshire Terrier, also known as a Pit Bull. Fascinatingly, the above graph is consistent with Fibonacci's Spiral. A series of bar graphs detailing the aforementioned characteristics such as age and breed would be the most effective way of representing this data. Simply a numerical analysis would be useful for determining how many attacks a year are occurring in these sites, and how many survivors exist. It would also be useful to determine what breeds survive these attacks. A binary survey could easily determine whether the common person perceives *C. latrans* as a risk for livestock.

Conflict Topic 3: *C. latrans* and livestock predation

To determine actual risk for livestock we must consider such a broad array of creatures such as sheep, cattle, pigs, goats and rabbits. The term livestock can be extremely subjective. By definition, it is a term for a living asset that is being raised for profit. This typically brings the image of open grazing land and cowbells, but I know farmers in the Southeastern United States who would consider the alligators on their property to be livestock, and farmers in the North who raise deer from conception to death.For the purpose of this study, a general list of livestock is built into the survey for the owners to select by type. This list includes cattle, poultry, swine, sheep, goat, and an 'other' category. Further, a comment section is offered for owners to identify indicators for their determination of coyote attack on livestock (fur, sighting, tracks, howls, scat, carcass details). A proposed point system would determine the likelihood that a kill was from *C. latrans*, within a reasonable margin. Data quality will be ensured by having recording individuals participate in an interview with one of the research hosts to determine legitimacy and accuracy. Each of the aforementioned factors counts as one point, and witnessing the kill and properly identifying *C. latrans* counts as two points. Reaching three points, or 50% of the criteria, will count the incident toward the overall statistic.

Conflict Topic 4: *C. latrans* and suburban/urban solid waste sites

The next point of conflict with *C. latrans* and human interaction is the creation, disposal and presence of solid waste in the form of trash. This is not a species specific problem, as in most places significant food waste left on curbs, in dumpsters, and in trash cans can be an opportunity for forage for bears, raccoons, and *C. latrans* alike. Similar to the others, this will begin with a survey to determine perceived risk.

Due to the fact that indicators are significantly reduced in trash spillage in comparison to livestock slaughtering, we must rely on eyewitness sightings. So that there is some measure of quality, witness statements will be cross referenced with existing population data regarding *C. latrans*. If the populations of *C. latrans* are above a certain margin, then it will be considered a positive sighting in conjunction with the witness account. A predicted issue with this is that individuals may falsely report their witness statements for want of being recognized in the study.

Conflict Topic 5: *C. latrans* urban habitat and reproduction

The next point of contention regards *C. latrans* breeding in urban centers. Although it is generally seen as less of an issue, it will quickly become increasingly relevant in coming years as urban sprawl continues to push into the range of *C. latrans*, and they are forced to find new habitats in which to breed. Again, we will begin with a binary survey to determine perceived risk. These areas are safe zones due to the fact that human populations generally possess the ability to prevent larger predators such as bears and big cats from entering, which makes them a more ideal place to raise young for creatures that are willing to situate with the steam vents, litter, and oil spillage of the contemporary concrete utopia. To determine whether or not this is an actual issue, further research is needed into the adaptations that are brought about in urban coyotes. It would be difficult to attempt to determine all populations of *C. latrans* within the limits of a city, and even more difficult to attempt to do so in a rural area. Initially, an idea of capturing these creatures in all six Sites, then analyzing their pathogen resistance and contractions was proposed. Two major influences helped to determine that this was a poor methodology for determining the home environment for these populations of *C. latrans*. To begin with, a recent study by Grinder and Krausmanm (2001) determined that there is no distinguishable difference between these factors from a biological perspective. Secondly, to complete this biological analysis would require the capture of these individuals. By the nature of that method, researchers would inevitably be able to determine the home location of *C. latrans* based on the location that the capture took place. This would only be applicable if *C. latrans* practiced migration and pathogen and contraction samples were able to assist in reaching a conclusion. A possible alternative is to utilize data collection systems that are already in place, such as disease tracking efforts involving *C. latrans* with the Fish and Game Department.

Perhaps in several years when multiple generations of the urban coyote have had a chance to reproduce we may begin to see microevolutions take place in their systems. For example, if a population of *C. latrans* resides in a neighborhood with a housing authority that requires all colored mulch to be crimson in color, could we begin to see the cryptic coloration of *C. latrans* shift to that pigment? This would certainly be the case if *C. latrans* was residing in garden beds, and making dens there. Individuals that are unable to camouflage in that environment would become targets, and would be selectively culled, leaving only *C. latrans* that express red coloration to survive. However, the safety zone created by human societies virtually negates the possibility of natural predators in an environment with a housing authority, and solidifies *C. latrans* as an apex predator. Until these microevolutions take place, it is unlikely that this study will be able to reach a confident determination regarding the question: is *C. latrans* using urban centers as safe zones?

Conflict Topic 6: Diseases in *C. latrans*

The topic of disease carries with it a heavy weight in the human population. This weight could be illustrated by an initial survey. Further, there are other points of contention that can be easily investigated into to determine whether or not they are an issue. Naturally, a survey would precede. These issues are of two major points: *C. latrans* infecting humans and animals with rabies, and *C. latrans* ending up in shelters. Statistics on both of these are widely available. Although *C. latrans* do end up in shelters meant for C. familiaris, it is not a common occurrence as *C. latrans* is rarely seen by humans during the day, and often show extreme timidness or fear in their presence. Rabies is not a major concern. According to the Centers for Disease Control, 92.7% of annual contractions of rabies were attributed to wild animals. In their ongoing study that began on the subject in 1967, many creatures have been added, including bats, foxes, skunks, raccoons, and even the mongoose. However, *C. latrans* does not even make their list.

Ethical research issues in this project are abundant. This makes the theoretical challenge of completing this research difficult, but it should not come as a surprise when you consider the wide breadth that the project covers. Aside from universal research ethics and standards, we must consider that we are conducting research beyond the borders of towns, cities, townships, counties, states, and even nations. Special considerations must be taken into account for this.

An additional issue faced by the project is that we compare cities to counties, which are unequal. However, for the sake of the project, it is possible to consider them equitable to one another. A final major issue that we see regarding this project is that the individuals taking part of the surveys are not objective. In fact, they will likely be completely biased based on their preconceived notions about *C. latrans*. Although issues for this project are abundant and the required funding might be equivalent to that of the cost to set up a mid-size avocado operation in southern California, the information gathered would be invaluable. Post-result discussion will explore these topics will aim to understand coyote relationships with humans and human perception.

Human-coyote standard index for determination of communal presence

A standardized index would be a valuable tool for the various research teams involved in this project to use. Utilizing a public and free program called ArcGIS allows citizen scientists to be 'sensors' and report data such as roadkill or foraging tied to geographic location. Further, it could be used post-study to evaluate the status of human-coyote relationships. Based on the results from the multiple surveys of interaction type and indicators, actual versus perceived risk will be analyzed and mitigation strategies proposed to reduce the human and *C. latrans* interspecies conflicts. This intervention could be a reduction of human influences, such as reducing traffic on a road with high incidents of roadkill. It could also be an effort to reduce *C. latrans* populations. The latter, however, has very little impact on actual population numbers long-term.

To this end, we will classify the research sites as 'wild' or 'urban'. Using the conflict topics, we will be able to determine the status level of the interaction between the humans and *C. latrans* in the area. The relationship status level will be classified as either minimal, moderate, or severe. Wild research sites may have a higher tolerance of interspecific interactions, given the larger space and nature of the sites. The factors will be comprehensive and compounding in a point system. This allows us to reach a determination of the status level on a spatial extent. However, it prevents us from determining the status interaction of a specific factor, instead favoring a broader presentation. However, the point system detailed below is on a three-tiered scale which is similar to the final index determination. This allows us to relatively determine the 'threat level' of a specific factor. This index will be measured for the duration of the study. The aforementioned surveys could potentially utilize a Likert scale for agreement or disagreement.

Roadkill will be determined by a certain number of reported incidents involving *C. latrans* per driver whose registered address is inside the boundaries of the site. For these sites, a ratio of drivers to incidents that exceeds 1:0.01 would result in one point. This frequency is one incident of roadkill for every 100 drivers within the time period. If this ratio reaches one incident per fifty drivers, or 1:0.02, it will count as two points. The ratio, reaching 1:0.05, would count as three points. Pet predation would be measured in a similar ratio. For every 1 out of 1000 domestic pets that have been confirmed kills of *C. latrans*, one point will be assigned. This is a ratio of 1:0.001. For every pet out of 500, or 1:0.002, two points will be assigned. Three points will be assigned for a ratio that reaches 0.005. The exact same quantifying factors will be used for the measurement of the livestock predation factor. On the issue of solid waste sites being menaced by *C. latrans*, our ratio must be significantly reduced due to the fact that contributing witness accounts are rare. One point will be assigned for every 1 witness site to 50 incidents of solid waste disturbance, or 1:0.02. Two points will be assigned for every 1:25 incidents, and three points for every 1:15. To determine the saturation of *C. latrans* populations, eyewitness sightings that measure one incident or less for the duration of the study would deal a singular point. Between ten and one sightings would count as two points. Ten or above sightings would count as three points. Positive, confirmed contractions of diseases as a direct result of *C. latrans* is our final factor. For every one of these incidents per 1000 diseases contracted from all animals a single point will be added. For every one per 500 animal-human transmissions, 2 points will be added. Every single contraction per 200 animal transmissions, or 1:0.005, 3 points will be added. A total of 6 or less points within an urban site would be classify the relationship as minimal. 8

points within a wild site would reach the same classification. Reaching a sum that is between 6 and 12 in an urban site would be classified as moderate, where a sum between 8 and 14 is the same in a wild site. A final sum between 12 and 18 in an urban site and between 14 and 18 in a wild site classifies the relationship between humans and *C. latrans* in that site as severe. It is at that point that interventions will begin to be considered.

Conclusion

Many ideas are perpetuated about *C. latrans* in modern day society. Some of these, like their tendency to spread rabies, are not built on a foundation of fact. These ideas are sustained through culture, but completing a large scale project such as this proposal would be involved to a point where such falsehoods are analyzed and brought to a point where they would be conclusively proven or disproven. In this proposal we were able to uncover that *C. latrans* was not a significant spreader of the rabies virus, but it would further the pursuit of knowledge about these creatures if this study were to be completed because of its range and the many human societies that would become the subject of it. Although this is only one point of contention, the others that were discussed would provide much needed insight into the significance of *C. latrans* in our 21st century urban, suburban, and rural communities.

This project is complex and costly. It is needed to finally create a formal presentation of the many issues that are relevant to *C. latrans* and human interaction. Data gathered will clearly define opportunities to reduce conflict and points of contention.

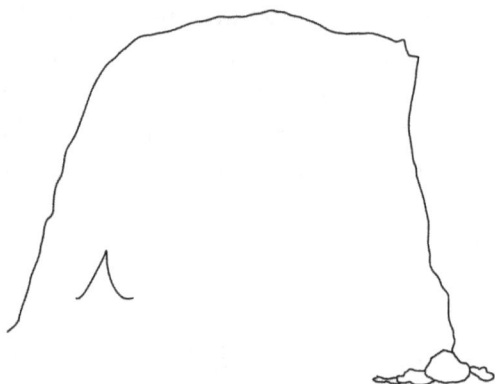

Marlow

MARLOW

"The wild hawk to the wind-swept sky,
   The deer to the wholesome world,
And the heart of a man to the heart of a maid,
   As it was in the days of old."
-Rudyard Kipling, The Gipsy Trail

I sit in a pseudo dwelling in a canyon outside of Moab. It was designed a few decades ago by the state parks system, complete with arrowheads inlaid in the brick. It was supposed to be a fee station for the nearby campgrounds. The design of the thing is precisely what would come out if the blueprints for every indigenous structure from here to Chaco Canyon were put through a shredder, then glued back together by an elementary schooler into a single page and adjusted to be up to code.

That being said, I'm still sitting here enjoying the space. The sun is setting and the crickets are beginning to come out and sing with me. I'm here with my car and my guitar recording a song I wrote for Cam. Music is a private thing for me, so I am a bit shocked when a man in a three wheeled recumbent bicycle pulls up.

"Howdy," I say, standing up.

"Hey, how ya doin," An older man says. He looks like he's been fist fighting the sun all day, and has only come home because he won the match.

"Good, how are you?"

"I'm good," He says. "Just headed home,"

"Is this…?"

"No, not this cave. The one up there."
The man sits on the ground and we introduce ourselves. "I'm Cedar,"

"Is that your real name? A trail name?" He asks. We share a smile. "In that case, I'm Marlow."

We speak for a minute about our mutual friend, Chris. Or Alex. Depends who you ask.

He looks at my vehicle, which has the letters "Power to the Peaceful!" painted on the cargo rack.

"Are you headed to The Land?"

"In a way, I guess, what-"

"No," He clarifies: "It's a commune at the back of this canyon." I pause for a moment.

"I wasn't, but now I just might be," I say.

"I'm asking because you look like you might've been." He says. I make a note for the future. "How about Cisco? You ever been there?"

"Yeah, I've driven through quite a bit, but I can't say that I've ever stopped to look around. Are there even people that live there?" I ask.

"Sure, a few folks. My friend Eileen runs the artist residency out there, you should stop the next time you're out that way. Tell her you're a friend of Marlow's, and you'd like the ten cent tour."

"I will…definitely do that." I say. He spends the next

45 minutes of lapsing sunlight exchanging his shoes as we sit in the dark together. I learn so much about this man. I learn that he has been living the seasonal life for most of his years, and that he writes, prints, and hand binds adventure journals. He's got an office in town that he rents. That's where he came from. A Moab man, living in a cave and writing. He inspires me, and makes it clear that I should keep living the life I am living, because there is nothing better than it.

There are no frills on this guy. An honest, sustainable and hard working man that shares his stories with the world. I help him push his bike up the hill into the cave. A massive repression into the sandstone, I cannot see to the back despite him holding a flashlight out. He invites me deeper.

"Is this the part where you kill me?" I ask. He laughs, but otherwise doesn't respond. He shows me his camouflage tent and food cache. "Do you ever get kids coming in here in the middle of the night trying to scare themselves?"

"Yes! Often. I still haven't managed to find a way to say 'hey there's someone in here', because by the time I say 'hey' they're screaming and running out the door." Marlow says with a chuckle.

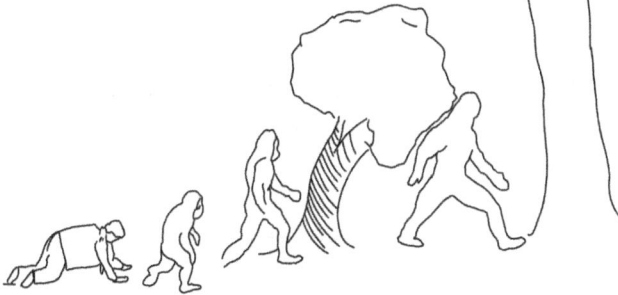

Achieving carbon neutrality through the lens of Juniperus monosperma & Sequoia sempervirens

Achieving carbon neutrality through the lens of
Juniperus monosperma **&** *Sequoia sempervirens*

Abstract

A carbon footprint is a useful tool for measuring part of your impact on the planet as a whole and in comparison to other members of the same society. Using this concept, this paper numerically analyzes what it would take to reach carbon neutrality by planting two different species of *Juniperus monosperma* and *Sequoia sempervirens*.

Every living thing on this planet has a carbon footprint, and it could be positive or negative. Carbon is the building block of life, and is essential for nearly any form of cognisance or locomotion. Humans have by far the largest carbon footprints of any living thing, which contributes to gasses being deposited into our atmosphere. These gasses contribute to the greenhouse effect, where they interact with solar radiation to contribute to global warming. There is a strikingly common misconception that trees can reduce carbon emissions. While this is true to an extent, the real reason that professionals advocate for the preservation of our natural forests is because of a miracle of arbor: sequestration. Most trees contain the ability to sequester, or store, carbon dioxide. This is where the misconception begins, because this is the extent to which most folks bother to understand the equation. The full story is that when the tree dies or is wounded, that carbon is released back into the atmosphere, further worsening the greenhouse effect.

With that being said, an excellent way to become more environmentally aware and hopeful is to take an analytical look at your personal carbon footprint, and how you can change it. These carbon footprint calculators are available online, all it takes is the tap of a few keys. A 2021 survey of 1,000 American adults between ages 33 and 40 concluded that 19% of this age group are not planning to have children. Although the declining state of the political hellscape and a collapsing economy were bound to be symptoms of late stage capitalism, this decline in parents may come as a surprise. Many factors could contribute to this decision, including a warranted increase in feelings of environmental accountability. This accountability leads to awareness of the natural impact of human life, particularly in places where there is a resource disparity in consumption versus actual needs. That is to say that many individuals in parts of the world, myself included, have more than they need in wealth of resources; food, water, electricity, and a manifest of commodities and conveniences that would be far too long to list.

Pair this feeling of responsibility that was scarcely expressed by prior generations with a decaying economy, and feelings of doubt and insecurity are bound to take place. Many people have great fear about their future in this environment we share, and have chosen not to bring children into this world for lack of suffering in the tumultuous tribulations that lie ahead.

I have this fear. Let me first say this: this project is an experiment, not a condemnation. I have meditated long and hard on this subject, played with numbers and consulted experts, which brought me here. A question: What if an individual could plant enough trees to be carbon neutral at the time of their death?

First, let us take a look at the region that this project will take place in.

The region I live in currently saddles the border between Utah and Colorado. A backcountry trail will start you walking from the Colorado River, through a deep sandy wash and between sandstone mesas as high as skyscrapers. Ten miles deep, you'll find yourself 6,000 feet higher in elevation and surrounded by an aspen forest on the slopes of the La Sal mountain range. Due to the closely intertwined relationship of these ecosystems and climate zones, I will speak about several of them so that we may understand how they interact to impact one another. This impact cycle tends to flow downward in elevation, following gravity.

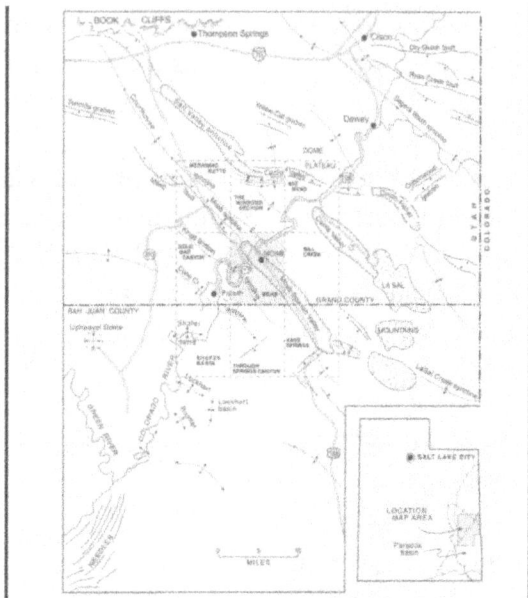

Figure 1, the 7.5 minute quadrangle of Moab, UT. This region on the Colorado Plateau is called the Paradox Basin, named for being the end of the watershed for the Paradox Valley further east in Colorado. That name comes from the maze-like formation of the Dolores River, which cuts perpendicularly through the valley rather than classically parallel. I reside across from the Cache Valley, in the north-eastern most quadrangle depicted. This figure effectively illustrates the many water sources at play in this complex environment.

Winter begins the calendar year here. The portions of precipitation from the end of the fall solidify their place as part of the seasonal imagery of the region. This paints a picture on the landscape on the peaks of the La Sal mountains. Here, the snow will remain until late summer. For most of winter, temperatures will hover around 25 degrees Fahrenheit during the day and drop down to single digits and occasionally negatives once the sun has set. This was a surprise to me--I had no idea the desert got this cold. Similar to most of human history, the settlers of this region live in direct proximity to our rivers, lakes and creeks. Due to the fact that these bodies of water nestle at lower elevations, most homesteads in this area find themselves in a valley or a canyon. This exacerbates the temperature reduction, as high cliff walls or mountains cut off sunlight and create a phenomenon locally known as a 'canyon sunset' or 'canyon sunrise', where direct sunlight ceases several hours before the actual sunset at a higher elevation. The medial time is filled with ambient yellow light.

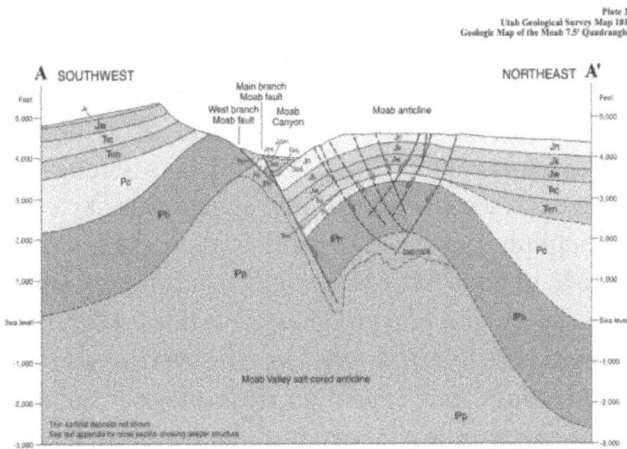

Plate 1
Utah Geological Survey Map 181
Geologic Map of the Moab 7.5' Quadrangle

In Figure 2, we can observe the salt-cored anticline of this region. Water action during this season and in the spring is a leading contribution to soil sterilization along the banks of ephemeral streams, as the water becomes super saline.

It is also during this season that our black bears remain in hibernation. Cottontails and squirrels remain as active as ever, foraging vicariously. The black angus cattle remain stationary in huddles except to feed...energy conservation is the name of the game for these ladies.

In the early days of spring come the rapid cycles of freezing and thawing. Melting snow and rain finds its way into cracks in the sandstone mesas, then goes through a few of these cycles. It is for this reason that early spring is the most common time to witness landslides and rockfalls, and also the most dangerous time of year to go hiking and climbing in these areas. Those that slept through the winter begin to awake and explore as the snowpack gradually reduces. In late spring is mud season, where most of the roads on the mountains become impassable except via monster truck. In most places, foot deep mud sloughs over the road. Further down, the snowmelts accelerate and collect minerals and topsoil, exposing substrate. This loaded water is an abrasive force to be reckoned with, for when it hits the weak sandstone it obliterates it into alien looking structures. This is the reason for many of Southeastern Utah's unique rock formations that seem otherworldly. Many fields of clear cuts left behind from the 20th century allow the floods to accelerate at ungodly speeds, sometimes uprooting entire aspens, junipers, and pinyon pines. As stated earlier, most folks around here live in the valleys. The average speed of a flash flood around here is 35 mph. This does not sound fast. In comparison to how fast humans have travelled, it is not fast at all. However, when you illustrate a bit with the idea that it feels like getting hit with a vehicle at that speed, you begin to understand why so many homes are destroyed and so many cattle are swept away. On the tail end of spring is the beginning of the hardcore rafting season. Temperatures during the day are around 50 degrees Fahrenheit, with little vertical precipitation. The floods can create rather deep and dangerous ephemeral streams, which are a favorite to traverse among hard shell kayakers. Chunks of ice six inches thick still populate the now muddy brown water, like marshmallows in hot chocolate. The water is far from mimicking that temperature, though, clocking in just above freezing. The raised water and obstacles from the flood create an intense nightmarescape for the unseasoned paddler. This is why the spring is the best time to train.

Early summer is truly sublime. With young wildlife in abundance and the snow gone, the classical perception of summer in the red rocks begins to take shape. The river drops in volume and returns to its emerald green color. The washes have just a few inches of water in them, and our local winged population is as loud as ever. Temperatures begin to rise and hover around 100 degrees. A stark contrast in temperature can be found in the water, which remains around 40-50 degrees still. Very little precipitation is present. More creatures come out of the woodwork on the caps of the day, choosing to avoid the scorching heat of the midsummer sun.

Late summer brings even more intensity from the sun, with daily temperatures soaring around an average of 115 degrees. Rock walls become unscalable, even for big horn sheep. Vegetation in raw, direct sunlight roasts and wilts. All but the deranged and the paid avoid being outside for a few hours every day. Catfish begin to die in the river due to the rising temperature, and can be seen floating on the surface of the water. They lack the metabolic enzymes to function at these increased temperatures, and only ended up in this section of the river because of the floods. An easy target for a bird of prey that does not want to work very hard. At this point in the year, river water is like bathwater. Rattlesnakes hide on the far sides of rocks, in the shade, waiting for hikers to step down before they strike. The cloudless sky from early summer disappears and brings with it clouds in the afternoons and the evenings; the beginning of monsoon season. Often, nights can be spent on top of mesas looking out at silent storms of magnificent purple heat lightning. More often, the clouds bring down heavy wind and rain which fill the washes and pools that have been empty since spring. Sandstone pits fill with water, which will become rife with brain-eating amoeba and protozoa once the sun hits it...or so they say. These are known as 'cowboy jacuzzis'.

In the fall comes the end of monsoon season and the beginning of hail, ice and snow once more. Temperatures drop, tourists leave, and animal activity increases again. This is especially true for the deer populations, who dive into the rut during this season. This is also when endotherms will begin to develop their winter pelage and shift their diets to a different seasonally focused diet. For example, deer focusing on woodier plants rather than leaved ones. I try to live as sustainable as possible, never using plastic utensils, cups, or paper plates, using a handkerchief, reducing my food miles and drive miles, buying vegan, buying sustainable products, taking short & cold showers, etc. I recognize that most people do not live this way, so this study will be based on the average American citizen's carbon footprint. A 2008 study by the Massachusetts Institute of Technology determined that even energy conservative Americans output double the amount of carbon than the global average. According to the Nature Conservancy, the global average carbon footprint, including CO_2 and methane, is 4 tons. The average American's is 16 tons.

First of all, a mass reduction is in dire need for reasons that I do not need to explain here. In fact, that goes to an entirely different study. Here, we will focus on the sequestration of my carbon, along with the carbon of three strangers. These strangers could be my partner and two children, they could be the paperperson, the garbageperson, and the grocer. They could be you and your family.

For simplicity's sake, we will add methane into carbon for one lump sum. If the average American produces 16 tons of carbon annually, then 4 people would produce 64 metric tons of carbon annually. Extrapolated to a (generous) lifetime of 100 years, this family of four humans would produce 6400 metric tons of carbon. Meanwhile, a family that falls into the global average only produces 1600. Now, onto the trees! Junipers, also called cedarwood, grow locally and are prime candidates for my Carbon Sequestration Autobank, your local CSA.

Although there are dozens of species of juniper, there are two that I will run into through the course of this project. The first is the Utah juniper, Juniperus osteosperma. The second is *Juniperus monosperma*, or one-seed juniper. To an untrained eye, they are challenging to discern. However, the key to proper identification lay in the name. J. osteosperma is named for producing multiple seeds within a single berry, whereas *J. monosperma* is named for producing a singular seed. Therefore, it is reasonable to assume that the berries of *J. monosperma* would be significantly smaller. This assumption is rooted in reality, as a comparison of the two berry sizes reveals. It is fascinating to note that the juniper 'berries' that are host to the seeds are not berries at all, but cones. These cones have evolved a wax coating to reflect sunlight and maintain water through drought and constant, extreme sun exposure. This may seem irrelevant, but it is in reality a key part of what will make this project a success. The process of fruiting is temporary, and results in seed dispersal at the conclusion of the fruiting season. Due to these cone-like 'berries', this project can be completed at nearly any time of the year that the ground is accepting. *J. monosperma* occurs significantly more frequently around me (it is also the one that is commonly mistaken for blueberries and eaten by tourists) so its seeds will be the subject of this study.

Cupressaceae, the family that Junipers belong to, can be observed on every continent excluding Antarctica. Most species in this family are shrubs or small trees, and most are monoecious, except the juniper, which is generally dioecious. Some junipers in the nearby Canyonlands National Park have lived up to 700 years according to the National Park Service. They generally do not grow to great heights, instead preferring to develop horizontally rather than vertically. Distributions of juniper in disturbed areas is reflective of relictual range. That is, few survivors are left from original development or culls.

Among the many remarkable abilities and survival strategies of the juniper is the ability to 'tourniquet', or isolate, a limb in times of severe drought or nutrient deficiency. This is why you can sometimes see a healthy juniper with a 'dead' looking limb.

The plant grows all across the globe, and has nestled its way into our culture in more ways than one. In Dutch, the plant is referred to as jenever, when shortened this word refers to gin. Gin is flavored from the plant.

Also known as 'red cedar', the aromatic compounds in the plant are often steam-distilled into an essential oil. Although the name may suggest otherwise, this plant is not in the Cedrus (Cedar) genus. The wood is red and is common for wardrobe construction, as it is said that the powerful scent can prevent the nesting of moths. Its wide distribution may play a key factor in the fact that it is widely used by indigenous communities, especially those who reside in the Great Basin. The ash of the tree has been consumed by Navajo peoples for generations as a rich calcium source. The twisted, knotting bark of the juniper has incredible compression strength that plays in tandem with a low weight. When lined with sinew to create tension, this has created an excellent choice in hunting bow for many people.

Now that we have established a model organism for the project, let's crunch some numbers!

The Cupressaceae family can be broken down into 7 sub-families. However, none of these subfamilies have ever been the subject of any legitimate or professional scientific data relating to carbon sequestration capabilities as far as I was able to locate. This unfortunately means that we will have to design and operate a workaround. All is well--this means we get to talk about California redwoods. Doing so will eventually allow us to determine the number of junipers that would need to be planted to neutralize myself and three others. I know how that sounds. If that's how I go out, that's how I go out.

In one of the aforementioned subfamilies lay *Sequoia sempervirens*, commonly known as the California redwood, giant sequoia, coastal redwood, or coast redwood. These trees are the carbon storing heroes of North America, mostly due to their magnificent and awe-inspiring scale. According to By Jessie Szalay, a science contributor, "Giant sequoias can grow to be about 30 feet (9 meters) in diameter and more than 250 feet (76 m) tall." These same adult trees weigh 1.6 million lbs a pop.

Trevor Nance, a geologist hailing from Duke University, has determined that one mature redwood will sequester 250 metric tons of carbon in its life. Using this, we can determine a weight-to-carbon-weight ratio r by dividing the lifetime sequestered pounds c (500,000) by the mature weight w(1,600,000).

EQ A

500,000/1,600,000=31.2

Or

r=c/w

Using this result, we can determine that roughly ⅓ (31.2%) of the total weight of a mature redwood tree is sequestered carbon. These trees are genetically similar to the juniper, meaning that this figure will likely bring us to a reasonable estimation.

This also means that the felling of one mature redwood potentially releases 500,000 LBS of carbon into the atmosphere.

Next, we must determine the weight of an adult juniper, then determine what 31.2% (r) of that weight is to determine the amount of sequestered carbon.

A 1982 study by Weaver and Lund led to the creation of a table that provides a comprehensive quantitative measurement for the weight to diameter ratio of junipers. This study determined that for every .98 cm of basal diameter, the total pooled weight (average of wet and dry measurements) is 2.26 kg.

Junipers have a complex growth pattern involving twisting, knotting branches that often diverge before reaching breast height. After extensive searching, 30 mature junipers within the aforementioned zone were located as suitable candidates. I used steel d-tape to measure the circumferences of these 30 candidates, then determined the sum of the 30. I then divided that number by 30 to determine the mean, or average. This average circumference was 133.8cm.

Next, we must use this to reach the basal diameter in order to utilize the weight ratio from Weaver and Lund. To do so, all we need to do is divide the mean circumference by π, or 3.14.

This determines that the average basal diameter among the sample group was 42.6cm.

Using this, we can now apply Weaver and Lund's number

of .98 cm to 2.26 kg to determine the average weight of a mature juniper in my area. Using this equation, we can discover that the average weight is 98.21kg. This number is far lighter than what I predicted. However, it can be justified in the fact that we live in the desert, this wood is not dense with water and contains air pockets, and these trees are not much taller than I. While it is true that some junipers can tower to massive heights, the sample group is among the common population. Although I am highly skeptical of the numbers presented by the 1982 study, it is the single reputable source for this data I was able to find that I can mildly trust. In the future, a more comprehensive study should be conducted to ensure the accuracy of this data.

Using the above percentage from the similar *Sequoia sempervirens*, we can determine that if a mature *J. monosperma* weighs 98.21kg, it will sequester 31.2% of its weight. Each tree will theoretically sequester 30.64 kg of carbon in its lifetime.

For simplicity's sake, we will not be running the numbers on the first few years of growth, as the numbers rapidly change and there is little data available to accurately reflect that change. Instead, we will only use the data on mature specimens. Additionally, we will begin working with quite big numbers in the next few paragraphs. In an effort to make this digestible, the use of scientific notation will be avoided.

In order to sequester the 6,400,000 kg of carbon created by myself and three others, I will need to plant 208,878 of *J. monosperma*. However, this is under perfect survivorship in the wild, which is impossible.

Jamie Williams, my mentor for this project, has a master's degree in agricultural education from California Polytechnic Institute, among a plethora of other degrees and certifications. She estimates that the survival rate of junipers in the wild is about 30%. This means that we must plant 70% more.

This means that in order to accomplish my mission of carbon neutrality by way of juniper, I would need to plant 355,093 trees. This means that if I plant one *J. monosperma* every single day of the year, it would take me 973 years to complete my mission.

Alternatively, if I planted redwoods I would need to plant a total of 26 without the wild survivorship consideration. With it, I would only need to plant 44.

The massive amount of junipers required for this operation is simply (and disappointingly) insurmountable to be considered for a renegade planting project that would reach the goal in totality. This is, perhaps, exactly the point. Even though the season is appropriate, I might have the time, and I am physically fit enough to accomplish this goal, this equation only counts toward four American lives. Let's pretend for a moment that this is an easy thing to do, and is accepted as a common initiative.

The 2019 census states that New Jersey has a population of 8.882 million individuals. At 1600000 kg of carbon per person, the lifetime footprint of everyone who currently lives in New Jersey is...the calculator application on my cell phone crashed when I attempted to input this equation. With a more robust calculator, we can determine that this footprint is 14,211,200,000,000 kg, or 14 trillion kilograms. To sequester this using junipers, we would collectively need to plant 463,812,010,444 junipers. With the survivorship consideration, we would need to plant 788,480,417,755 or 788.4 billion trees.

The canopy of a mature juniper is generally greater than a square meter, but for the sake of this exercise we will pretend that the canopy is equal to exactly that. The total amount of square meters in the state of New Jersey is 22,608,000,000. If we assume that 100% of this area is land-based and plantable (which it is not), we would need 35 New Jersey's to accommodate for the carbon damage caused by those that live there. This goal is unsustainable, unrealistic, and downright impossible. Instead, it is imperative that we reduce our consumption.

Given that I lead a sustainable lifestyle and given the heartbreaking result from a moment ago, let's run the numbers for me to neutralize myself and 3 others based on the global average footprint of 4 metric tons per person. By multiplying this to account for others, four global citizens equal the carbon footprint of one American. Due to the fact that our numbers are nice and whole, all we need to do is reduce our previous final result by a factor of ¼. With this number, I would only need to plant 88,774 junipers. This is unrealistic on a financial and time scale for me. More importantly, doing so would create a variety of ecological impacts, many of which unforeseen, which I am not qualified to approve as I am only one member of this landscape. The impacts this kind of operation would have on the ecosystem would be unprecedented and likely landscape altering. Having come to this conclusion, I have decided to plant the 44 sequoias.

To do so, I have traveled to an undisclosed location in USDA plant hardiness zone 9. It was in a stand of already existing *S. sempervirens*. For the safety of myself and this project, no further information regarding the area will be given.

I had four days in early July in California to complete this project. After consulting with the renegade tree planting locals, I began by first selecting a juvenile specimens within a healthy ecosystem. I rounded the figure of 44 up to 50 to allow for a higher final product number. From these juvenile specimens, I used loppers to sever healthy cuttings about the length of my forearm. After being severed, the 50 cuttings were soaked in a bucket containing a room temperature solution of root growth hormone which contained both Endomycorrhizal and Ectomycorrhizal fungus.

After 6 hours of soaking, it was dawn on the second of the four days. The knowledge I obtained about successfully completing this project in such a short amount of time comes from three local gardeners in the area that were keen on my mission. They suggested that after this, I should spray the cuttings at the stem and at the leaves every 45 minutes. So began the exhaustive cycle of babysitting my new children for the rest of this long weekend. Due to the fact that this species requires a day/night temperature cycle, my original consideration of doing this at an indoor location was no longer an option. I alternated using two different spray bottles, one with an acid focused compost tea given to me by one of the gardeners, and one with the root hormone. The cuttings were laid on a tarp in the sun. Every cycle, the cuttings were rotated 180 degrees. At night, I covered the cuttings with an additional tarp, but still sprayed every 45 minutes all night. The second tarp was removed at dawn. This process continued until dawn on the final day, day four. At this point I evaluated and inspected each specimen in detail, and determined that four of the specimens were no longer viable. They were composted.

The remaining 46 specimens were planted in an area that had had a prescribed burn just 7 weeks prior to my arrival. This allowed for less competition among the shrubs and a thinner canopy for a promotion of sunlight for my project. I planted the cuttings about four inches deep, or ⅓ of the total length of the cutting. They were planted in soil that had been soaked in both the rooting hormone and the compost tea for maximum growth potential. Unfortunately, my economic and employment status will prevent me from continuing this study directly and from returning to determine success rate in the near future.

Although this was an extreme workaround, I believe it is a testament to how we must be creative about how we adapt to solve our problems. Things are hardly ever simple when you know the whole equation, and persistence will bring you to new conclusions that you likely did not expect in the least bit. Reducing our personal carbon footprints is just the beginning, systemic change is still needed.

S. sempervirens is serotinious, meaning that the dispersal of its seeds is entirely dependant on a trigger. Out here, this is fire. Forest fires in this environment clear ground cover and make phytonutrients bioavailable. By evolving to release seeds upon the presence of a fire, sequoias effectively ensure that their seeds land in a 'safe spot'. For this project, we'll be attempting to create a safe spot by making nutrients as available as possible and selecting a location without much low ground cover. A fire has recently happened in this region, and I likely walk among the young and still invisible seeds from the last dispersal. I do not think I need to draw the comparison between the germination of sequoia seeds and human life through the lens of fire and of the coyote, it is already available to you. Adapt, survive, thrive. Crucibles are hot, and they make strong swords.

Jane

Jane

"How can a deer tell when a leaf falls silent in the forest? She hears it breathing differently."
 Richard Bach, *Running from Safety*

Down 128, river road,
By the only other ranch of its kind.
A white pickup coming the opposite way, way under.
Staring in the rearview mirror.
Oversized everything, polished.
Urban cowboy. You know the type.
A blind bend,
She rests in a panic.
Greets me with a sniff,
Yellow=====================exposure.
A group watches.
There is no blood yet.
I grab someone, we glove up.
Primary Assessment: Primary Suspicion: shattered rib, broken leg.
A carry over to the baking dirt,
Push the tumbleweeds out of the way.

A bed of dried cottonwood beneath her nose as I perform
Secondary.
Pouporii.
He rides up, blonde mullet.
How do I?
The hatchet throwing place in town. He also works there.
Her head rests in my lap while we wait.
What's your name?
Pushes legs, trying to envelop herself in me, I think.
Maybe asking Adam for a rib.
Big black eyes.
I hold her tightly.
I think she has a chance, I really do.
The rancher asks me to do it.
The radio in his hand gives me permission, but Grand
County Sheriff's Office is on their way.
45 minutes.
An expiration date, down to the minute.
She can't speak English. I explain in a different way.
I try to stand, she pushes into me and forces back onto my
lap.
She isn't ready. Who could be?
A few moments ago she wasn't thinking of this
Just happened to meet the wrong man.

This whole Sentinel thing, it'sits about respect.

He could have at least finished the job.

The ones with the badges could finish it too. But I know that
the weapon of the 21st century predator has capabilities that
theirs do not. They both are centerfire, both eject the brass,
and both exhale the sulfuric Breath of Death.

I can't believe that I've got to do this again.

The lack of respect and responsibility has brought us to this stage once again, with one standing over the other. One with all the power.

The distinction, I tell myself, is that my weapon delivers mercy.

I pull the bullet from my coat pocket and insert it into the broken barrel.

Click.

She looks at me. She's heard that before, somewhere less dangerous than this.

I tell her to get up and run. But there isn't a place she could go where she would escape them.

This canyon boxes out.

I want to pick her up and carry her to somewhere she can be safe.

She can't even stand up. She can't breathe. The sun cooks her, even now.

But I know that no human will harvest.

I don't know what else is bleeding, I'm not an MRI.

Her clock is ticking. There's no way around that.

This rancher, this urban cowboy, has handed her a death sentence and they won't even look when I complete their order.

How dare you?

I speak to her and give her all the time that I can.

They're almost here. There's no way to know if they would look. No way to know if they would tell her it is time. Give her last words.

I know that the 21st century predator will.

I'm sorry, Jane. I've given you all the time I can.
I don't aim.

The force at this range slams her head into the bramble, springing back up. She vibrates into a seizure.

The radio crackles. "Sheriff's office says to hold off on shooting her,"
"You need to leave," the rancher tells me. But I can't. She's still here. And I'm in there, like before.
Still parting.

Her wet, rudolph red nose presses into the cottonwood leaves, breathing hard, like she was the final time she ran.

A good smell to end with, I hope.

…

I still drive by her a few times every day.
Every day her corpse becomes a little more deflated, a little more hollow.
These necrotic cells transfer to me.
These days, I wear her like armor.

I wanted to bury her.

I settle for deliveries of desert sunflowers.

I had to go. That wasn't something for me to do.

I hope that the urban cowboy has to commute past her.

I hope that he has to see what he did.

I hope that he has to see

what he forced us to do.

And I hope that next time he has the strength to finish what he started.

Destabilization Factors of Human and Coyote
Communities In Relation To Climate Change

Destabilization factors of human and coyote communities in relation to climate change

xiii. Squirrels eat the birdseed. Who is more deserving of the meal?

Claire Wineman, *Thirteen Ways of Looking at a Bird*

Introduction

Canis latrans can be an exemplary tool for critically analyzing the success or failure of human societies. With a development of blame that began with our ancestors, the coyote has seen the evolution of the modern human and has often been blamed for the many pitfalls that plague our communities--both ancient and modern. After the eradication of *Canis lupus*, *C. latrans* began rapid expansion that mirrored the growth of colonial America. Now, the coyote lives with us in almost every city in North America, a fact that contributes to a variety of points of contention. New strategies can help to reduce these points, but a shift in the zeitgeist of 21st century consumption is necessary.

The coyote is integral to many ecosystems in North America. As urban development increases, both human and coyote populations expand. In more ways than one, *C. latrans* is reflective of contemporary issues we face as we accelerate deeper into a climate emergency. By exploring the desert landscape we can draw back the curtain and expose many of these issues. The eradication of *C. lupus* can also provide insight into the modern understanding of *C. latrans* as we attempt to reduce points of conflict.

What is a desert?

By far the most frequent comment I receive while guiding clients in this region is "it looks so green". I would classify Moab and its surrounding area as a desert, but this begs the question: what exactly is a desert?

According to Merriam-Webster (n.d.), a desert is "arid land with usually sparse vegetation, especially : such land having a very warm climate and receiving less than 25 centimeters (10 inches) of sporadic rainfall annually". Most outdoor professionals will agree with this measurement; however, it is imperative to note that this precipitation statistic is trending to vary widely in both directions as climate change continues to destabilize these regions. For example, U.S. Climate Data records Tucson, Arizona's precipitation last year as reaching 11.92 inches or 30.2 cm. Much like 'global warming' was rebranded to 'climate change' to incorporate cooling action, we must take into account that some deserts are getting drier and changing, while others are getting wetter and suffering. Is Tucson no longer a desert?

Common Desert Adaptations

The desert is an extremely challenging place to live. Most

creatures must adapt physically and behaviorally in order to survive in these places. Many traits allow the flora and fauna in these regions to thrive. An example of this is cutin, a hydroxy fatty acid produced that coats most forms of cactus that are found in the Americas. This can be found on the giant saguaros closer to the equator and in prickly pear cactus that share much of the same range as the coyote. The waxy coating aids in the reflection of sunlight and retention of water by way of reducing transpiration action. This reduction of transpiration is the same evolutionary adaptation that encourages most desert plants to have needle like forms rather than leaf like forms. There are exceptions to this, though, such as the singleleaf ash (Fraxinus anomala) and the cottonwood (Fremont cottonwood Or Populus x canadensis). However, it does not take a keen eye to observe that both of these semi-common plants occur under special circumstances. Singleleaf ash is rarely observed outside of sky island woodlands and high chaparral, and it would be incredibly difficult to find a cottonwood more than a few meters away from a perennial water source. This explains why the cottonwood is able to survive with an abundance of leaves. The singleleaf ash, however, is often found a great distance from waterways and produces leaves as well. Fraxinus anomala is different from the others in its family because it produces only one leaf per stem, which effectively reduces the surface area enough to cope with minimal water and maximum sunlight. Unlike many of the leaves that appear in spring, those of the singleleaf ash remain until the fall where they become part of the beautiful amber landscape along with the cottonwoods.

Cottonwoods are essential to the native ecosystems of the desert. Their roots penetrate deep, aerating soil and allowing the percolation of water deep into the horizons, all while stabilizing river banks and preventing erosion. These trees can grow up to 90 feet tall and are commonly the sites of rookeries for great blue herons. The rookery provides a nesting station and home base for these herons to hunt and raise young out of, and often host extended family groups for many miles in either nautical direction. Additionally, their branches are among the most common building materials for beaver dams. On top of all this, cottonwoods tend to grow with an abundance of cavities that are prime real estate for raccoons, squirrels, chipmunks, and owls. Despite the obvious importance of this tree, stream channelization, grazing, and clearcutting have played a deadly role in the last two hundred years of history for cottonwoods. Today, forests of cottonwoods have been reduced 90 percent from their native occupation. Further, several other adaptations allow plants to thrive in this challenging environment. Many of them have the ability to become dormant and 'awake' in the presence of moisture, others produce thorns and spikes to prevent creatures from attempting to attack and access water stores.

Other species well adapted to these conditions and desert flora include many of our snakes and lizards, as well as a significant population of small rodents. Creatures such as Ord's kangaroo rat (Dipodomys ordii), go their entire adult lives without consuming a single drop of water. Instead, they have the remarkable ability to absorb nearly all the water that is contained in their solid diet of nuts and seeds (Williams, p. 87). A true desert survivalist, the kangaroo rat is exclusively nocturnal and seals off its burrow during the day to reduce energy and moisture that would otherwise be spent keeping it cool. By producing exceedingly concentrated feces and urine, the creature subscribes to an effective survival trait that many other creatures in low-moisture environments utilize, such as the camel. Further, the creature utilizes a specially shaped nasal passage that recirculates outgoing breath to reduce water lost through vaporization. It is named the kangaroo rat due to the way that it bounds when stressed--on hind legs.

The Clever Coyote

Although the coloration of the coyote adapts to a lighter tan to match its environment in the desert, a greater number of differences can be found between urban coyotes and wild coyotes than can be found in wild coyotes at opposite edges of its range. Previously, weWe have just discussed the adaptations that have made several species of flora and fauna successful in the deadly desert landscape. To become the 21st century predator, the coyote has had to make virtually no physical changes. Instead, the creatures change their behaviors. They become exclusively nocturnal. They stay close to water sources. They ration their food.

Is it better to be successful by nature, or is it better to achieve this through hard work and discipline?

Cryptobiotic Channels

A staple of most desert ecosystems is biological soil crusts, also known as Cryptobiotic soil crust. This crust is extremely common across the globe in arid environments because it forms a symbiotic relationship that is mutually beneficial for its own survival as well as the survival of surrounding flora. Cryptobiotic soil is not one organism, but a community of 15 or more types of fungi, mosses, lichen and bacteria that work together to provide these services. Blue-green algae, also known as cyanobacteria, is the main component in most of these crusts. Microcoleus vaginatus is perhaps one of the oldest life forms on the planet and composes 95 percent of the biomass of Utah's biological soil crusts. Further, it provides multiple ecosystem services.

One ecosystem service that this soil crust provides is stability. It, by excretesing filaments into the surrounding soil bed followed by an excretion of a mucilaginous membrane that binds soil together, roots included (Williams

p.22). These filaments promote aeration and water penetration. Further, they allow light to penetrate beneath the
surface helping to allow microorganisms, which promote
soil health, to be cultivated. This action is developed by
the production of a polysaccharide called the Microcoleus
sheath, which activates when wet and weaves around all
particulate matter inside and on the ground such as; stones,
root balls, grasses, mineral deposits, or an unfortunate
earthworm. The production of the mucilaginous membrane
is fully effective even when completely dried, despite the
fact that it is produced exclusively in the presence of liquid
precipitation.

The silty soil left from years of hydrologic erosion
dominates this landscape.. The naturally compacted and
fine textured nature of this soil prevents much water from
being retained, especially when a great deal of the precipitation comes in the form of monsoons, which cause flash
floods. According to the Environmental Protection Agency,
the average speed for a flash flood is 2.7 meters per second, or 9 feet per second. The speed of this water makes it
challenging for the soil to absorb the liquid. A function of
the biological soil crust is to produce a complex landscape
for this water to travel through, acting as a sort of pinball
machine to slow water speed across the surface. This reduces run-off to improve water infiltration. This aids in the
ecosystem service of water retention and storage provided
by the Microcoleus sheath. When liquid precipitation is
present, these roots can swell up to 10 times their original
size and hold the moisture even after the water event is
complete.

Moreover, the lichen and bacteria inside these crusts
are nitrogen-fixers, meaning that they digest atmospheric
nitrogen. This is among the key symbiotic relationships that
make these soil crusts essential. The soil crusts process this
into bioavailable nitrogen for surrounding flora. The major-

ity of the plants in this region lack the ability to fix nitrogen themselves, and perish without a nitrogen fixer. This is the same equation that we can observe in the classic three sisters example. Beans aid in the production of the cyanobacteria, which fixes the nitrogen present in air pockets in the soil and in the atmosphere, and makes it available for the surrounding plants.

A fascinating note is that the soil crust is actually a replication of the surrounding area on a smaller level. The crust reflects the fractal patterns in nature, as there is a degree of self similarity found at all levels of scale. If you look closely, arches, mesas, plateaus, buttes and canyons are abundant in these cities of cyanobacteria. Shape translates to function as the complexity of pattern produced by Cryptobiotic soil crusts serve as a safe site for seed dispersal. This is primed with exposed pathways into depths via the sheaths, available water, protection from wind and animals, and darker surface colors to attract more sunlight.

Form alone does not determine the function. Dark soil color on the surface of mature Cryptobiotic soil serves another purpose: reducing surface reflectivity. When the silt and sand is exposed due to a lack of Cryptobiotic soil albedo, or surface reflectivity, the amount of heat being redirected off the surface increases. This creates columns and pillars of thermal wind that extend into the atmosphere, repelling the cooler altocumulus clouds.

As a byproduct of the water retention abilities, the Microcoleus sheath becomes extremely tensile. This trait allows the crust to aid in erosion prevention and hold together through extended periods of drought. While it possesses extreme strength in this way, it lacks any form of compressional strength. In A Naturalist's Guide to Canyon Country (2000), Williams draws the comparison to that of a bicycle tire. When on a rim, the tire faces hundreds and hundreds of miles of use and abuse. However, applying compressional strength by standing on the tube or placing it within a vise will immediately dispatch it. This compressional strength is what is required to withstand the trials and tribulations that have been brought to the desert with increased tourism.

Due to the fact that this soil crust is essential for our desert ecosystems, its abundance should not come as a surprise. Increases in visitation and tourism in these fragile landscapes quickly leads to the destruction of Cryptobiotic soil. It is incredibly fragile; one bootprint, horse step or tire mark easily kills the soil. Most soil crusts take several hundred years to become fully established. Sharp increases in visitation unfortunately do not correlate with sharp increases in staffing, signage, and budgets for our protected spaces like our state and national parks. This leads to an extreme disparity between traffic and available resources. Most installed park interpretative content (signage) contains installation dates in the early 2000's, which is the most recent time that park staff numbers were increased if we exclude the re-hires after the government shutdowns and the advent of the recent pandemic.

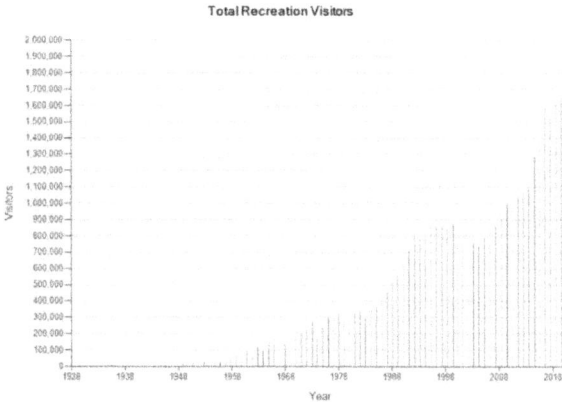

Total Recreation Visitors

In Figure 1 above, this graph of Arches National Park provided by the National Parks Service illustrates that around
the time that this signage was implemented and the total
number of park staff to be hired was determined, annual
visitation was about 750,000 visitors. Last year, despite the
virus, annual visitation reached an all time high of 1,650,000
visitors. It is unreasonable to assume that the same staffing
and interpretive & protective resources is sufficient for more
than double the amount of annual traffic. A 2000 study in
Arches determined that after being stepped on, the water retention capabilities of Cryptobiotic soil crusts were reduced
by over 90%. Although online and paper resources have
increased significantly in the previous decade, it is evident
that additional in-person park staff are needed to protect
these landscapes (Figure 1).

Fire is an important part of many ecosystems,
including many deserts, and can help illustrate the deli-
cacy of Cryptobiotic soil. NHowever, natural fire cycles
can be disrupted by invasive human activities. Fire needs

three resources to survive: heat, fuel, and oxygen. Plants are similar, though the resources are different. They require nutrients, water, and light. If you remove any two factors from a fire, oxygen and heat for example, your flame will be extinguished. The very same thing is true of the lifeforce of Cryptobiotic soil. Footsteps compress the crust to a point where the nutrient cycling stops and water penetration is effectively mitigated.

Further, large scale destruction of cryptobiotic soil can result in habitat fragmentation and can literally alter weather patterns. As mentioned previously, trampling cryptobiotic soil destroys the naturally dark color and exposes the lighter colored sand, increasing albedo. This increase in surface reflectivity creates a column of warm air, which repels water-dense cloud cover. The reduction in natural cloud cover increases temperatures and decreases precipitation, which begins a perpetual positive-feedback loop of drought. When the drought is broken, biological soil crust is not present to aid in mitigation of flash floods, which become more violent and powerful and wash away more vegetation, which further reduces the available water mass, which increases albedo in this cycle. Due to the fact that it is difficult to identify before the 50 year mark, crypto is often continually trampled in its younger stages. Additionally, once trampled cryptobiotic soil takes between 50-250 years to reach maturity if the affected area is small (williams). Larger areas of crypto have never been studied during recovery, but it is thought that the reconstruction period is extended based on the amount of surface area trampled.

Further, the habitat fragmentation caused by following social trails in areas where Cryptobiotic soil can be a leading factor of wildfires. Our native grasses and shrubs are designed to populate the welcoming landscape provided by the crust and simply lack the caloric power to penetrate compressed soil. This opens an opportunity for invasive grasses to populate. A disturbance ecologist, Steve Warren, has spent over 35 years studying damage and recovery to Cryptobiotic soil crusts at the USFS Rocky Mountain Research Station. Warren works closely with Larry St. Clair, a lichenologist at Brigham Young University. St. Clair states "Now with the invasion of non-native annual grasses you have the fuel to carry substantial and intense fire across hundreds and thousands of acres, which decimates both the native plant and biological soil crust communities." Cryptobiotic soil crusts can be indicative of both the health and the human impact in an ecosystem.

The Colonial Connection

When I was a boy, I would stare at the dark woods behind my house with fear. Fear of the wolves that we all know lurk in the humid and hot woods of New England. This fear did not come from dogs, which I love and always will. Rather, it came from stories. From the "Three Little Pigs" to "Beauty and the Beast", wolves have been used for millennia as an exemplum through which elders can teach children life lessons, such as to not wander off on their own.

For colonists in the Americas, the forest was a dark and terrifying place where evil lived, which is not too different of a perspective than that of my childhood. The Puritans, after being exiled, built tight communities in which they could worship and fight off starvation together in The New World. "The edge of the wilderness was close by. The American continent stretched endlessly west, and it was full of mystery for them. It stood, dark and threatening, over their shoulders night and day".

Due to the fact that North America was a place of religious exile for the Puritans, it is reasonable that they considered the place to be violent, dangerous, and unforgiving. It is perhaps for this reason that the forest became a place for the Devil himself to reside. To further their fear, there were others already there. The wilds were full of strange and foreign flora and fauna that was little understood to these farmers. "The New-Englanders, are a People of God settled in those, which were once the Devils Territories; and it may easily be supposed that the Devil was Exceedingly disturbed, when he perceived such a people here accomplishing the Promise of old made unto our Blessed Jesus (Mather, 1693).

With this quote, we can see the illustrated viewpoint of these terrified rye-eaters; the woods belong to the Devil, and we live on the edge. Therefore, it would not be unexpected for the Devil to want to harm us in this place. The breathing creatures that live there live under him, and therefore must be as evil as he, creatures and people included. With this viewpoint in mind, picture yourself in a foreign land, completely unfamiliar to you. You are an agent of peace, but carry a smoothbore musket which you are unfamiliar with. At a range greater than a few meters, your weapon is worthless. Your mission is to protect your fellow settlers, children included, and your crops. Without the security of these, the population is doomed by the next harvest season. Now, picture this: the sun sets. Strange and giant trees sway in the wind, carrying voices. A frightening sound pierces through the sound of the twilight insects, sending a chill through your heart and your spine. The sound is a howl from *C. lupus*. All that protects you are wooden walls. You will get no sleep tonight.

Witch hunts aside, it is logical why a Puritan would want to kill the wild dog upon the first instance of attributing that haunting sound. This viewpoint is one theory about the origin of the hatred for the wolf that was expressed for so many generations after the first sailboat landing on North American shorelines.

The Eradication *of C. lupus*

This viewpoint is shared in papers, journals and writings by many respected individuals, including the author of the first comprehensive guidebook of ornithology (Birds of America) John James Audobon. The modern day Audubon Society is also named after him. In his journals, there are over 30 mentions of the creatures. In the vast majority of these, he is either referencing clothing made of wolf skin or he is speaking on killing the creatures. In doing so as a respected naturalist, the way was cleanly paved for extermination campaigns to begin when settlers started livestock operations that were jeopardized by the canids. Writings such as the following piece taking place in the Ohio River Valley excused the sympathy that many farmers and ranchers experienced. Here is an excerpt from Jon T. Coleman in reference to an entry in Audubon's journal, "During the fall, a pack of wolves had robbed [the farmer] of "nearly the whole of his sheep and one of his colts." For him, it made sense to devote his winter labor to digging pits, weaving platforms, hunting bait, and setting and checking his traps twice daily. The animals had injured him, and "he was now 'paying them off in full.'" Audubon's reaction to the slaying of the wolves is less understandable … The ingenious pit traps amazed him, as did the fearsome predators' meek behavior and the childlike glee the farmer took in his work. The violence Audubon witnessed, however, did not shock him. Watching a pack of dogs rip apart terrified and defenseless animals was a "sport" both he and the farmer found enjoyable." (Audubon, 2016).

Hunting Methods

Although quotes from Audubon make these issues seem archaic, this assumption could not be further from the truth. On April 27 2021, Idaho Governor Brad Little gave the final signature to approve a bill that allows the killing of 1,500 wild wolves, totalling about 90% of the state's population. Just 19 years ago, the Endangered Species Act delisting agreement was signed into effect that brought wolves off of the endangered species list in the state. This agreement numerically identified the minimum number of wolves in the state as 15 packs. With about 10 wolves in the average pack, this means the minimum population size on a state level would be approximately 150 wolves. The agreement states that federal management standards for rehabilitation would be reintroduced if the total number of packs was reduced to 10. However, little tracking information is available for this 'cushion' that 50 canid lives are attributed to. The bill that was passed allows the population to plunge to the minimum level. "Lawmakers who sponsored the measure said they want the state's wolf population reduced to the allowed minimum of 150 to reduce attacks on livestock and to boost deer and elk herds" (Ridler, 2021).

It is well known and understood to ranchers that wolves hate the smell of humans and will actively work to avoid it. In fact, wolves are still hunted in modern day Russia utilizing strips of soiled human clothing atop poles (fladry poles). Multiple hunters will work together to form a perimeter around one or more wolves and close them in with the ultimate goal of killing them once they are trapped in a small enough area. Similar to the coyote but in a less pronounced fashion, wolves can sometimes be found integrating into more urban settings. In these cases, the fladry pole method is virtually ineffective due to the fact that the odor of humans becomes a background scent for the wolf.

Other alternative hunting methods include utilizing birds of prey such as eagles trained to immobilize a wolf while the human hunter catches up to execute the animal (Graves, 2007). This process is incredibly time intensive, as it only allows for one kill at a time and the bird must be trained extensively. Other animals, such as the Kyrgyz and Borzoi breeds of C. familiaris have been selectively bred for this purpose.

Once a tag is purchased, a hunter is then permitted to hunt an unlimited number of wolves on a single tag. If no hunter has a bag limit and the state has a reputable number of current populations, how will it be recognizable when the state's population reaches the minimum number of packs? Further, the bill that was passed allows private contractors to be hired to eradicate the creatures. It allows them to utilize trapping, snaring, and even helicopters. It also allows the utilization of night-vision goggles, binoculars, and scopes. Additionally, it permits the animals to be hunted from ATVs and snowmobiles. Such circumstances increase the chance of false identification and increase the chance that *C. latrans* or C. familiaris will be killed by mistake. Additionally, the law also allows hunters to kill newborn pups inside of dens...so long as they are on private land. "Michael Lucid, a biologist formerly with Idaho's Department of Fish and Game who helped write the state's wolf management plan before the new law, says big herds of elk don't necessarily indicate healthy ecosystems"(Ridler, 2021). But, they do indicate profitable ones.

Coyote Eradication

As discussed, the endemic range of *C. latrans* was vast, and was surrounded on most sides by the territory of *C. lupus*. This reiterates the competitive nature of the relationship between the two species, with *C. lupus* clearly forming the dominating and defining role by physical outperformance.

Once the hunting campaigns began against *C. lupus* during the manifest destiny period, their territory was reduced to a fraction of its original size. Once the wolves had vacated, this left a vacuum that *C. latrans* was more than happy to fill. Inside this vacuum was an easier life with abundant land on which to expand and reproduce, fresh game to consume, and in the absence of competition from what once was their greatest threat. This allowed a booming expansion of *C. latrans*, without restriction inside of this new range. With no balance system in place, the only thing left to stop exponential growth and expansion was humans. It can be inferred that the indigenious communities that had already settled in this area would have spotted the massive exchange in canid populations as out of the ordinary, whereas first time pioneers were unfamiliar with this territory. It is likely that they would not have been cognizant of the change, mostly due to the fact that the canid exchange occurred at the same time that these new settlers were expanding their territory as well. Due to the fact that the white settlers of the American West were likely the descendants of the original colonists, it is likely that they had a great fear and hatred toward wolves. By proxy, these bitter feelings likely projected onto the coyote. In fact, at the time they called both types of canid wolves. The names these new settlers used reflects the native territory of these creatures, where *C. lupus* is called the timber wolf and *C. latrans* is called the prairie wolf.

When the east coast settlers first made their way west, they brought with them livestock and the supplies to homestead. These new territories were wild when compared to the idyllic brick of the eastern cities and ruralities around Boston, New York City, Bar Harbor, Charleston and others. Prior to the advent of public lands, the Bureau of Land Management, and the idea of purchasing private property, livestock was allowed to roam freely and graze any which way. This is the intent of branding, tags, and collars. This practice still exists today, but a nominal fee of $1-$4 USD per animal must be paid to the overseeing agency if it is to be done on public land.

Grazing practices that utilized public land resulted in decreased supervision to livestock among ranchers. In these lapses of vision, sometimes even cattle and sheep dogs were unable to prevent recurring and often violent attacks by the endemic wolves. It should not have come as a surprise. In ecosystems where wolves are apex predators, can they be expected to resist the temptation of new prey that is quite literally being bred to be unintelligent, calorically dense, and slow? The result was the annihilation of herds of livestock by wolves for several decades. In retaliation, the first wolf eradication campaigns began.

When moving into these new territories, pioneers and ranchers saw many of the same issues that they thought they had quelled by eradicating the wolf. They utilized many of the same methods in an attempt to exterminate the prairie wolf.

The eradication of *Canis lupus*, the wolf, paved the way for the largest incident of mesocarnivore exchange that has been seen in modern human history and perhaps since the mass extinction of historic megafauna at the conclusion of the last glacial maximum (Meachen, 2014). *Canis latrans* readily filled ecological niches left vacant by the wolves. Latrans, being significantly smaller than lupus, quickly fell into the role of killing fewer livestock than their predecessor and instead favoring to feed primarily on carrion and smaller mammals. Nevertheless, the killing of livestock continues to this day and is the primary reason for which coyotes are seen as enemies of ranchers everywhere. Further research needs to include an examination into whether or not coyotes are a significant threat to our precious meat industry. David Williams, a Washington native, geologist, hero to me and former ranger in Arches National Park, says "No one has conclusively proven that coyotes do extensive damage to livestock; an individual may go on a killing rampage, but as a species coyotes are not significant predators of sheep or cows. In reality, their consumption of jackrabbits and rodents may help improve the range" (Williams, 2000).

Livestock Death

It is commonly known that most cattle do not lead nutritious lives, but instead are often fed cheap grain that is extremely different from the diet of their ancestor, the Auroch. This creature lived in southern Eurasia during the beginning of the Holocene. It is important to note that with the advent of agriculture being popularized, caloric stockpiles begin to take shape for humans and livestock alike. Prior to this, the few cattle that were kept as livestock led lives where they grazed on wild plants, not cultivated ones.

From 53 scholarly research projects, James B. Russell with the Agricultural Research Service in the USDA along with the AAAS have confirmed some major findings on these types of diets in cattle. The purpose of feeding cattle high grain diets, typically 50-90%, is because grain ferments faster in the rumen of the cattle, making more bioavailable phytonutrients in a shorter timespan. The simplification of the fermentation process in a ruminant such as a cow could be compared to how a human consuming a smoothie, which is already mechanically digested, allows the human to obtain nutrients faster and with less effort than consuming fruits and vegetables in their raw state.

Unlike smoothies, high grain diets contain fiber in amounts that are significantly less than in a wild diet. This results in less physiological regulation of the entire digestive tract, and often results in the accumulation of acids in the rumen. Without this necessary fiber, cattle are stripped of usable forms of amino acid chains, as well as protein and vitamins that are necessary for a healthy lifestyle. Additionally, a lack of fiber prevents the occupation of essential acid-digesting gut microbiota. Further, carbohydrase and amylase are two more enzymes that are lacking in grain-rich diets. These enzymes specialize in starch digestion, another necessary part of metabolizing the calories you consume. Without these enzymes, bacteria in the gut are given the opportunity to take advantage of the biologic imbalances and overpopulate. Without the presence of the acid digesting enzymes specifically, an accruity of acids collects. Similar to human stomachs, this can cause ulcers. The ulcers create a biologic gateway through which these bacterium can travel directly into the bloodstream, and create abscesses in other organs. In these high-acid environments, bacterium like Escherichia coli, commonly known as E. coli, naturally select to survive acid shocks. When this inevitably transmits into the beef that ends up on the table, the E. coli bacteria will not be killed in the high-acid environment of the human stomach. Another bacterium that can cause issues if unregulated is Clostridium perfringens, which allows for the healthy digestion of food in most mammals, especially ruminants. However, high grain diets can lead to uncontrolled populations of the bacterium, which can quickly overpopulate and have lethal effects. This polypeptide enterotoxin, when consumed by humans, can cause food poisoning. It is also one of the bacteriums responsible for causing multiple sclerosis (MS) and Baló's concentric sclerosis, as well as gas gangrene. Though the infection caused by the overpopulation of this bacterium in cattle is less studied than in humans, it is the leading cause of digestive related death in cattle behind salmonellosis, Cryptosporidium Infection and septicemia caused by Escherichia coli. Further, antibiotics are commonly used to treat these issues in cattle. This also kills probiotic bacteria, and alters the once natural state of the microbiome. In 2015, the FDA determined that approximately 80% of antibiotics were used in veterinary medicine. Moreover, these antibiotics fed to animals penetrate into most soft tissue in the body, which is what is consumed. This means that if you are a regular meat eater, there is a high chance that you regularly have residual antibiotics in your system. This constant presence of drugs selectively promotes drug-resistant bacteria, which contributes to many contemporary issues revolving around pandemics. Additionally, a 2017 study conclusively determined that this constant presence of antibiotics significantly raises the risk of weight gain and obesity by eliminating regulatory probiotics that are naturally present (Dutton, 2017). A large cow does not necessarily mean a healthy one, but it does mean a profitable one.

In the aforementioned Cattle Death Loss Report, the total number of predator based deaths in 2010 was 219,900, with 116,700 of these being attributed to the coyote. However, deaths related to "digestive problems" totalled 505,000, nearly five times that amount. Further, the aforementioned bacterial issues impact many organs, including the lungs. The same report details 1,055,000 deaths attributed to "respiratory problems".

With these statistics, it is difficult to imagine why so much attention is given to the coyote when it is responsible for a disproportionate amount of deaths when compared to the diet that is fed to the livestock. However, it is much easier to blame a creature that has been hated for generations than it is to blame the corn and wheat.

Compensatory Reproduction

As mentioned, the pioneers attempted to utilize the same strategies for the coyote that had worked to exterminate the wolf. However, this had the opposite effect, promoting the growth of more coyotes. Coyotes demonstrate a unique and powerful biologic trait known as compensatory reproduction.

In stable coyote packs, only two members of the pack actually reproduce. This is known as the alpha pair. This stabilizes the population and makes growth and regulation of the group predictable. When *C. latrans* mortality with hunting increases, pack member size is reduced. This results in a destabilization of the pack dynamic and increases breeding pairs. When the creatures are hunted the killing is sporadic and could eliminate members of the pack on any level, including pups and yearlings. Due to the lack of understanding of these dynamics, members from neighboring packs could be killed together. The result of this is the formation of a new type of pack, a pack of nearby refugees and survivors that band together. This pack is unregulated and inexperienced with one another, which promotes a lack of understanding about who the alpha pair is, and promotes breeding of all mature individuals in the pack rather than two of them. Litter size multiplies, and so do empty stomachs. The natural balance of surrounding prey animals is skewed, and the biomass available to feed the influx of pups is insufficient. This is what leads packs to kill livestock and domesticated animals. To summarize, killing *C. latrans* multiplies pack sizes and necessitates the death of nearby domesticated animals for *C. latrans* to survive.

This survival trait is what makes *C. latrans* perhaps the most adaptable creature that currently walks the earth, that is willing to do whatever it takes to survive even in the face of extermination, poison, and mass death. This is the might of the 21st century predator.

Traction Failure

It used to be that significant enough factors could cripple human civilizations. However, modern technology has brought us to a point where we can effectively produce artificial survival. A human body can be kept 'alive' for decades after neural activity has ceased.

On July 31st of 1809, a reunion for the revolutionary war Battle of Bennington took place. This battle was named after the nearby town of Bennington, Vermont. General John Stark, a revolutionary war hero, could not appear at the reunion due to declining health. Instead, he sent a toast by post. The toast reads "Live Free or Die; Death is not the worst of evils.".

When I traveled to New Hampshire for the first time as a boy, I saw the quote from Stark on every license plate as it overwhelmed my imagination. Often shortened to "Live Free or Die", this is an exemplary quote that embodies the state of capitalism and democracy in our contemporary world. If we are not free to pursue whatever we wish while trying to eliminate the consequences, then we ought to die. I believe this is the viewpoint of many barons that rule and regulate our economy today. In history, this was regulated by natural factors. Stockpiles of food, when too large, would be destroyed by rats or mold. Armies of men would age and would no longer be capable of going to war. Without water pumps, how does one stop their sprayed monoculture farm from flooding? These factors are no longer regulatory because we have reached a point of technological advancement that allows for artificial survival. This planet suffers because we have the technology to remove the consequences that would otherwise prevent it.

30% of human populations are subject to heat waves exceeding safe living standards for over 20 days each year (UNEP)

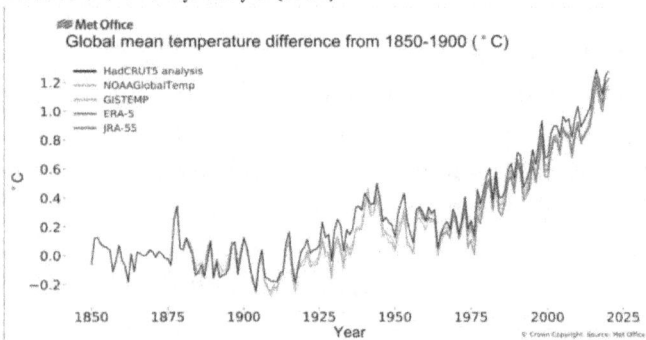

Met Office
Global mean temperature difference from 1850-1900 (°C)

This graph from the MET Office illustrates the mean temperature difference from multiple sources beginning in 1850 and going to present day. Temperatures are irreversibly rising as technology 'advances'.

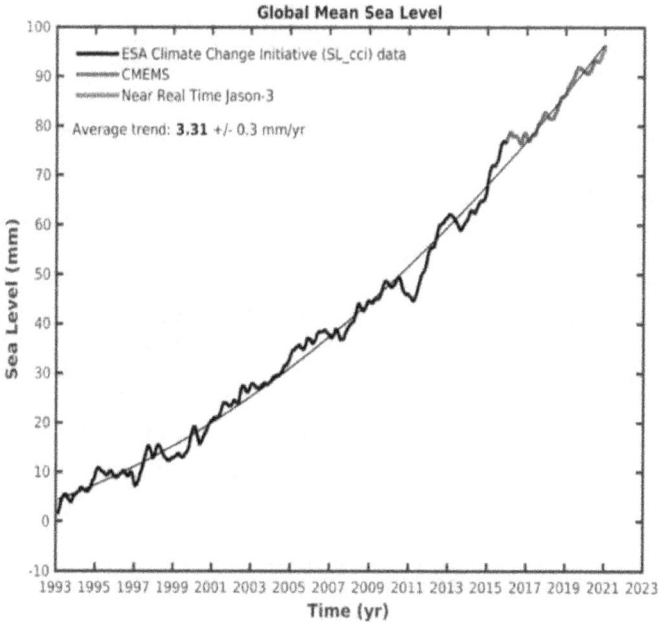

Global Mean Sea Level

From the World Meteorological Organization, we can see that these rising temperatures are melting the global ice reserves and causing sea levels to rise. This causes severe flooding and will soon wipe seaside communities off the map. Notice how the presented graphs all follow the same projection. According to the WMO, "The six years since 2015 have been the warmest on record. 2011-2020 was the warmest decade on record."

Professor Petteri Taalas, the Secretary-General of the World Meteorological Organization, said "All key climate indicators and associated impact information provided in this report highlight relentless, continuing climate change, an increasing occurrence and intensification of extreme events, and severe losses and damage, affecting people, societies and economies. The negative trend in climate will continue for the coming decades independent of our success in mitigation. It is therefore important to invest in adaptation."

The 21st century predator has advanced to a point where obtaining food, power and life is virtually no challenge if you are born in the right circumstances. However, this lifestyle is clearly not sustainable based on the above findings, as well as a plethora of others that were not mentioned. We are, at present, working to adapt the climate to work in harmony with our desired lifestyles. However, we must return to doing the opposite as we have always had to do to survive. Not doing so will result in a mass extinction event on a scale that humans have never been witness to. It will not be quick, but slow and agonizing. Even those that have the wealth, resources and power to avoid exploitation will be among those that perish. We need to change the way we live, because death is not the worst of evils.

Points of Contention

As a review, the main points of conflict between human and coyote populations are the deaths of domesticated animals including livestock, coyotes exploiting trash, coyotes breeding in urban centers, and rabies.

Reducing Conflict

Based on the remarkable trait of compensatory reproduction, it is clear that killing *C. latrans* will only exacerbate the issue at hand. Instead, much like the theory that lay opposite of "live free or die", we must change the human things to reduce our issues with coyotes.

Most livestock operations occur on land that is part of the native range of coyotes. Reducing the size of these operations would reduce the occurrence of attacks and deaths from coyotes. Of course, doing so would require consuming less meat to reduce demand. Many of the domesticated dogs that die due to coyotes are working animals trained to protect livestock. Reducing livestock operations would also serve as a reduction of deaths involving C. familiaris.

To further reduce these deaths, investing in larger and hardier breeds that have experienced fewer generations from their ancestor, *C. lupus*, could help. Smaller breeds like the chihuahua and shih-tzu lack the physical prowess to properly defend themselves against a predator like the coyote. Further, allowing these animals to live more outside would likely increase adeptness in self defence and threat detection, increasing survivorship. Keeping animals like the dog indoors for most of the year except to relieve themselves, even in cities, is actively preventing them from being prepared when urban coyotes eventually reach your stead.

The sole purpose of rooting through trash, from a coyote's perspective, is to locate food. A reduction of food waste and introduction of a compost based system would prevent coyotes from being interested in trash cans. For city dwellers, garbage disposals or countertop compost may be the way to go. Community gardens offer a place to take this compost that is safe, reliable, and effective. A community garden where beds are based on a compost donation is an excellent idea. For those that are incapable of such solutions, bear-proof garbage cans could be an option for you. We are long past the days where loud sounds and streetlights will keep coyotes away, due to the fact that the human range has expanded into the territory of the coyote in such a way that they have nowhere else to go.

Coyotes breeding in urban centers is a complicated issue. They are safe zones. The idyllic solution would be to introduce a different apex predator that would disqualify these areas as safe zones, but this is unrealistic and would exacerbate many of the issues we have already discussed. This issue cannot be eliminated, but only mitigated by making more sustainable cities and reducing the expansion of urbania.

As discussed in the research proposal, the spread of rabies by *C. latrans* is less than negligible.

To further reduce points of contention, it would be useful for the common person to familiarize themselves with how to identify a coyote. This could reduce incidents of misreports and help individuals more effectively aid in conservation efforts, potentially saving the lives of *C. latrans* and *C. lupus*.

Tomorrow

We all play a key role in making tomorrow a better place for ourselves and for children, even if you choose not to have them. It is reasonable to be frustrated with large corporations and even whole companies that are still seeming to fail to make the necessary adaptations it will take to survive the climate emergency that we have entered. There are both scientific and media driven campaigns that promote the idea that reversing our environmental disasters is going to be the result of individuals making critical lifestyle choices. For example, a New York Post article (Sparks 2019) claims that watching Netflix for 30 minutes generates "1.6 kilograms of carbon dioxide into the environment — the equivalent of driving almost 4 miles". For the sake of this point, we will ignore the point that this is an incredibly situational and subjective number. Some communities generate power from coal, others from natural gas, etc. While this carbon number is backed by multiple other news sources, the fact that it is such a prominent headline speaks volumes. The majority of the articles that cite this number are advocating for a decrease in usage of streaming services to promote a reduction in carbon footprints. This is excellent advice. As outlined by the stakes of our situation above, we need to do everything we can to mitigate the emergency. However, articles such as this dominating the media bring attention away from issues that are, in reality, significantly more relevant and threatening.

According to the Environmental Protection Agency, 29% of 2019's carbon emissions are attributed to transportation (6,558 million metric tons). This transportation includes the diesel fuel it takes to haul away your trash to the landfill, to drive your cases of plastic water bottles from their manufacturing plants, to fulfill your 2-day shipping option from Amazon. My point is this: individual choices such as Netflix are not the problem. The consumption of our system is.

The average distance that an orange takes to get to your plate is 3,643 miles. We can use this statistic to draw a direct comparison to the above listed 4 mile equivalent of carbon produced from a 30 minute television show. From the same source, a piece of steak travels 4,129 miles to reach the plate of the average person. These mileages are based on an average origin to destination search from thousands of people, beginning in 2017 and operating to the present. While reducing electricity and internet usage will help, articles like the aforementioned one are abundant and unhelpful--they are little more than red herrings. The core of these issues lay in our consumption. As I write this, our ocean is literally on fire once again.

The things that we can realistically do to mitigate our carbon footprint are on a systemic scale, which makes them unprecedented and frightening to look at critically. Reducing the amount of episodes you watch on Netflix is tangible and, for most folks, an easy adjustment to make. Reevaluating your entire diet and where your food comes from is another task entirely. Reducing vacations to exclude airline and cruise ship travel would be unspeakable, and forget about ditching plastic utensils, paper plates, and disposable water bottles. Asking for a change on that level would be asking the majority of people in most developed countries to quite literally change their lifestyle. When presented with the dilemma of making lifestyle sacrifices or death, *C. latrans* is happy to make that transition, time and time again. Humans are apex predators, the top predator in the food chain in a given ecosystem. The same can be said for coyotes in a great deal of ecosystems. To remain at the top, the 21st century predator can no longer afford the luxury of choosing between "live free or die". The 21st century predator must adapt to survive, or die.

With that being said, there are still a great deal of things that an individual can do without uprooting their life, and indeed without making intimidating decisions. You can choose what kind of food you eat-- eat organic whenever possible (yes, that label does mean something), and reduce your food miles by purchasing food from your local farmers directly, from the farmer's market or a CSA program. You can reduce your carbon footprint by targeting high-resource parts of your diet, such as meat. If you eat a lot of meat, try Meatless Mondays in your family and purchase organic, grass-fed, grain-free, cruelty-free and non-GMO cuts. Doing so ensures that the meat you are eating is free of the cow-killing diet we discussed earlier, where a great deal of meat is simply wasted. By making choices that positively involve these labels, even though you are consuming meat you are promoting healthy livestock operations. In short, buying clean can save lives, even if you aren't vegan.

There is so much hope. There may be smoke in the air, but blue skies are behind it. We can effectively change much of our landscape ourselves, but children are the key players of this system overhaul. After all, they will be around tomorrow. We will not.

A 2020 study by Cambry Baker, Susan Clayton and Eshana Bragg statistically analyzed the extent and impact of climate anxiety in children. Baker, an environmental psychologist with the College of Wooster, discovered results that indicate that anxiety about the future of our climate in children is significant.

A section of the study compared challenges to respective positive actions taken by surveyed parents and teachers about their children and students.

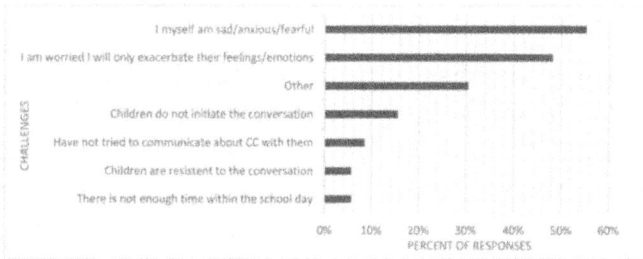

In figure 4 above, we can see the survey results of both parents and teachers on the subject of discussing climate change (CC) with their children or students. These results indicate that a great deal of children may be sheltered or prevented from learning about the realities of our climate emergency. This is the world that they will grow up in. Preventing them from understanding this reality ensures that they will be ill-equipped for the leaders that tomorrow needs.

In figure 5, we can observe results pertaining to reactionary positive experiences on the subject that includes children, parents and teachers. Numbers here indicate that a greater number of individuals reported more positive experiences than challenges, overall. By far the largest positive experience reported was taking positive personal action. Doing so for children, and supporting them to act on their own, is a powerful tool that will make all the difference in the coming years.

Anxiety about our ecosystems and the survival of our species and lifestyle can be a terrifying thing. Clearly the honor system of ecological responsibility that has been the status quo of the last two hundred years is outdated and ineffective. The above graphs, however, illustrate that there is hope. Although a great many generations would rather "live free or die", it seems that the children of today understand what it will take to ensure that there is a tomorrow.

Nevertheless, this does not mean that we should relax for a moment and sit back to let the Little League team handle our plastic waste problems. They will not get a chance to unless serious and immediate action is taken today. There are so many other ways that an individual can mitigate their impact. For most of you able to read this book, simply existing in this landscape as a human is inherently damaging, wasteful, and resource intensive.
I am of the opinion that traveling to a new place should warrant a great deal of intention and research. Just as you investigate culture so as not to offend anyone when traveling to a new place, you should do the same with the ecology. An excellent example of this is our Cryptobiotic soil here in Moab. Online resources are abundant. Ask a local. Know where you are going. By recreating outdoors, you invade a space that isn't your home. A friend, geologist and colleague, Lo Nickell, once said to me that she pretends that she is perpetually on a first date when she recreates outside.

Would you throw trash on the ground? Would you walk somewhere you aren't entirely sure is on the path? Would you hoot and holler, or play loud music? This creates an aura of nervousness and intention behind every action. There is a misconception that we own land, and it is our right as humans to do with it whatever we see fit. Perhaps this 'first date' feeling, even though it may be uncomfortable, is how we should feel about being outside. I think that this is a fantastic lens through which we can view how we inhabit outdoor spaces. Listen to the land, because it speaks to you. Open ears will change perception.

Humanity as we biologically know it has only been around for about 200,000 years. Our flat earth has been around for about 4.5 billion years. This means that humans have been around for only 0.0044% of history. If we interpolate the age of the planet with the amount of time that humans have inhabited it into a 24 hour day, at 10:55 PM the first dinosaurs arrive. It is not until 11:59:59 that humans appear, the last millisecond before midnight.

Look for ways to be smaller. Take colder, shorter showers. Ride your bicycle or walk whenever possible, invest in small (or large) scale solar to cut your electric grid reliance down. Utilize the windows in your house, and try to be comfortable using the natural temperature cycles of the day instead of blasting the heat or the air conditioning in your home. Spend the few extra dollars to get a travel cutlery set and reusable water bottle. Get a handkerchief and washable kitchen towels. Use these instead of paper towels and tissues. Look into getting a bidet. Build a home compost system. Try purchasing only used clothing, even as gifts. When your things break, try to fix them or repurpose them into other useful things. If your shirt rips beyond repair, you've got a new set of rags next time you work on your car. Plant trees. Be outside and be present and be mindful. We are all part of this natural world, as it is part of us. It is time to adapt to the changes that are coming, and the changes that are already here.

Today's children are growing up in a dangerous world where pollutant haze is more common than fog and fewer umbrellas fit on the sand every time they go to the beach. They hear airplanes instead of birds, and wildfires are just another thing that prevents you from seeing the stars. Educating and enabling for resilience is critical for the survival of our species. Like the coyote, we must adapt or die. Talk to your children. Talk to someone else's. Give them the tools they need to succeed. They are tomorrow. Our world is burning. The era has come to adapt and cultivate resilience. Let's start today.

Together At The End Of The World

When you say '9 out of 10 wildfires are caused by humans', all I hear is 'there's a bear somewhere out there that knows how to use matches'
- Unknown

JUNE 9

Mike Hawk drives Cam and I through the La Sals. We're in his black pickup truck, but he'll tell you that it is actually a very dark green.

Our hiking bags are in the back seat. The air up here is wet and refreshing, a sharp contrast to the desert floor where we live. We're headed to Doe Canyon, one way or the other.

We drive past Max Lane and Cedar Lane, named for us long ago.

The road here is blocked off, but the man in uniform won't tell us why. All three of us are adept at reading maps, we find another route with no problem. Only, the other route is rife with dead ends. Another hour or two on dirt roads leads us in circles. Gate after blocked and locked gate. A place in the woods that reads 'The Blue Hole', but this is a drought year. Nothing more than a grassy depression in the woods.

Frustration when we continually have to reroute. We're never going to get there. Mike chain smokes in the driver's seat while we drive. Cigarette in one hand, beer in the other, the steering wheel somewhere in between.

Mike and I stand near an open gate with another no trespassing sign. The headlights miss us and project out into the woods. I shine my headlamp briefly, trying to conserve the battery for the rest of the trip.

The three of us agree. The sun will be up in 6 hours. Let's do it.

The topography through here isn't very different, but the road is in worse condition. A more natural one. It is clear that nobody has driven it since the snowmelt.

A large ranch building, there, out in the darkness. We slow down to make less noise. At least 10 other trucks outside. We don't know where we are. This isn't on the map. A light flicks on, we floor it.

Gravel shoots up from the tires as we speed down the long, long driveway. Nothing but darkness behind us and--wait, headlights. Mike pushes the vehicle harder, faster around the bends. The back tires release from the gravel and skid laterally on a turn.

Maybe we could fell a tree behind us to block the path? The beam of the pursuer's lights cuts through the aspen forest, a searchlight.

God, if a deer jumps out right now we are dead.

We meet an intersection, Mike chooses a direction without hesitation. I hear his gas pedal hit the floor. We accelerate, both leaving the dark and entering it.

JUNE 10

We awake on the side of the road, Mike left us here after the brief escapade. I pull down the bear bag, my breath condensing in the dawn. Today marks the beginning of Cam and I's trek through 30 something miles of Utah mountains, following the Trans La Sal trail from peak to peak. Beginning in Doe Canyon, our trail will bring us to where my car, Bongo, is parked north of Castle Valley.

The maps we use are a collection & collaboration, and anything but cohesive. Some of the maps are modern, some simply pamphlets with suggestions. Others still contain photos from the 1970s, when they were officially printed. In reality, the Trans La Sal Trail does not exist. Rather, a collection of smaller and shorter trails connect and intersect it. The challenge will be to see which of these trails are still readable, and which have been swallowed by the mountain.

It is green here. Too green, like when you close your eyes for too long in sunlight and the red of your eyelids shifts your color perspective. Something feels not right. The trail climbs high, soon we find ourselves in fields of cow pies and needing to rest at 11,000 feet above sea level.

The air is thin.

Do you feel more winded if you try to do cardio on an airplane?

The sun is high overhead, we hike on a level part of a steep embankment, surrounded by pines and black soil. Snow crunches beneath our boots. We stop for a drink of water, that's when we first saw it.

A plume of smoke. Small at the base and fanning out to fade into the atmosphere, like a meteoroid perpetually falling.

Not a meteorite. There's a distinction.

There's a worry that the fire isn't incredibly far away. It doesn't seem to be moving, either. We make this advanced calculation in the 20 minute snack break.

There's service here, too. We text Mike and tell him what we see, and check the fire report.

The first time I saw the words. The Pack Creek Fire. 400 acres and growing. 0% contained.
There's no wind. It'll stay in the valley. The plume is rising completely vertical until it catches on a current in the upper troposphere.

And then, maybe, it is headed back the direction we came from. The rest of the trail rises in elevation and brings us closer to the lakes, Medicine, Oowah, Warner, Clark. We'll be hiking past most of them, actually. We reason for a moment.

In those moments it rarely feels like your decision could impact anything in a large way. The future is made of small things, small things that when we do them never seem to have the traction or the power to bring big change. Looking backward, the big things are almost always made of thousands of smaller ones. Or maybe one specific smaller one, like continuing north.

If we head south, back down the mountain and the way we came, we'd have at least another 30 miles to cover on dirt roads before we reached any pavement, and even then there's no telling when the nearest passerby would come, or if they would even pick us up. The lakes are closer, more achievable than a conceived stranger at the end of our trail. The smoke is going back the way we came, anyway.

Until the wind changes 45 minutes later, blowing eastward and up the talus slopes. It is far away. The lakes, Oowah Lake, at least, have to be between us and that smoke, and that's our safest option. We pick up the pace, teetering on the line between fast walking and running.

Uphill, down, bounding. The trail disappears entirely here. Is that a bear? A cow? It's starting to smell more heavily like smoke. Still can't smell well, not after the virus. We stand on logs to survey above the tall grass, beating back the bush with our trekking poles. 40 pound packs digging into our hips and shoulders, sweat dripping. Get to the lake.

The sun sinks lower.

The smoke climbs higher. Tannish white now. Without that color, it would almost look like a cloud taking over the sky.

A cabin, nearly swallowed by alpine grasses and purple and pink and blue and yellow flowers. Intact, hitching post still outside. Glass missing from the windows. We can't keep going at this pace. The door is locked by a metal coat hanger over a nail. Easy enough to lockpick. The floor is cracked stones. Tabletops covered in rusted tools, cabinets stocked with brands and labels I've never seen. A military duffel bag hangs from the ceiling, stuffed full of a sleeping bag. Keep off the rats. A mattress in the corner, reduced to springs and empty glass bottles all over the place. It is a clean space, with a broom in the corner. We breathe. Check the map. Slow is smooth, and smooth is fast.

That smoke is getting closer. Is it at the lake? Too much distance to cover headed south. The fire moves, we feel it in the air pressure. On these mountains the fires can move 10 miles per hour or more. If it is on our heels, there's no way we could keep pace and get to a safe position if we head back toward the trailhead. We've already traveled 10 miles today, most of it in an anxiety-induced hop.

I've heard of a mine, or maybe just a prospect. The La Sal Pass Mine. 3 or 4 miles closer to us than Oowah. Achievable. Doable.

Okay. Let's do this.

A sigh. We push hard.

An overlook, the fire is massive. Closer than ever before and incinerating treetops like nobody's business. The smoke travels further toward us, and will soon be over our heads.

We drop down and traverse through Hell Canyon, aptly named. Cam falls, bends her trekking pole. That's what we get trying to run in loose soil, high grass, downhill with exhaustion and 40 pounds on our backs. Others have had it worse. That doesn't matter in this moment.

She's okay.

Halfway to the mine. We breathe in the smoke. It gets darker out. It's only the evening.

A trough. For some calf-cattle operation that has long since been abandoned. Being reclaimed by the mud, just like her. It has green algae water in it. A little bigger than a bathtub.

We can both fit is the thought that is exchanged without words.
And be boiled alive?
I picture popping heads up to swallow smoke, clinging to one another, popping back down under like turtles.

No, we can make it to the mine. We have to make it to the mine. There isn't really another choice.

Would the mine be better? Safer? I picture frantically ripping off ancient boards of wood until we can crawl into the shaft. The red smoke pulling oxygen from inside. It is cool and wet and clean in here. Trapped methane ignites with an ignition source. A tree could fall and block our exit. So many unknowns.

The aspen forest spits us out onto a rocky fire road.

The sky above is shrouded in a veil of thickening smoke. The sun like someone spilled blood over a light bulb.

Hell canyon.

Nothing short of a 4x4 diff lock sway bar lifted nitrogen-charged piggyback reservoir shocked FIPK'd brush shielded monster could make it up this road. That is, except us.

Because we have to.

Just around this bend, it has to be. This bend? That bend? This hill is gruelling. A rock slips. On my knees. Almost a broken ankle.

The same, over and over again. It isn't the rock's fault. Muscle failure. I fall again, my leg collapsing beneath me.

We reach the mine. Or, where it is supposed to be.

It is even marked on our map. But, there's nothing here.

Game over. Right?

We hike up the road, back down it. All around.

The bushes here are brambly, tall. Unrestrained and unrestricted. I lean over the edge of the road, leaving my pack and hat behind. The loose ground falls through beneath me, delivering me lower into the canyon. Maybe the entrance is down here?

I rip my shirt. I rip my pants. I rip my skin. Nothing. Nothing but bushes. No entrance, no shaft, no pile of rocks no hole no equipment. End of the line.

I claw my way back uphill to the road, pushing my ligaments and these green branches to their limits. What will snap first?

Cam grabs my hand and rips me free, back onto the road. Conditions are worsening.

I look at her. Tears of loss? Tears of acceptance?
I know her better than that.

The smoke ebbs and flows, sucked in and out of Hell Canyon, aspirating.

We are inside the lungs of Moab, Utah.

White ash lands delicately on her tightly pulled, frizzed hair. We hold each other.
This could be it. This could be the last few minutes.

The smoke blankets the valley below us. Cut off from the back.

Her eyes are wet. Mount Tukuhnikivatz, affectionately Tuk, stands indifferently. Not much taller than us.

What can you see up there, big guy?

You can see our whole world.

Please, tell us what to do.

Which way to go.

Please.

Deliver us.

Our foreheads touch.

Part of me wants to give up. To stop and let it take me, because that would be easier than going on. Anything would be. To let it take me, but not let it take us.

I think of her family, mine, our friends and our life. I tell myself.

Do it for her.

I don't know, because I've never asked. In her eyes, I then saw something. A reflection.
Did she have the same thought?

She can do this alone, as can I. Our strength comes from the togetherness of the thing.

Not sadness, not loss.
No.
Hers are tears of ferocity.

I picture a fire burning inside me, brighter and hotter than the one we now face.

Armor up.

The only way out is through.

The death march takes us rhythmically around another pass.

We head for a spot of water marked on our old, old map. Nothing more than a puddle. We sit and refuel, eating energy bar after energy bar is like eyedropping gasoline into a screaming engine. I think I could eat my own weight in carbs right now and still be hungry. These are belt driven machines.

The lake. Not enough time to relax. We can't let the fire cut us off.

Get to the lake. We can hide in the park service restroom there, they're supposed to be fireproof. We can go for a frigid swim in the turquoise water as the fire consumes everything around us. And we could hold each other and breathe shallow and clasp wet sleeves and say this-water-is-so-damn-good.

We push higher in elevation to an overlook with an adjacent rock field. Alpine grasses and wildflowers dance in the wind.

We look down on the mountainside. The lower half is obliterated, black and reeking.

When I was a boy, I never understood why I should use the red crayon to color fire, and why it was the same color as blood.

I get it now.

This isn't the orange fire inside a pit.

This fire is alive like no other I've seen. It breathes and penetrates the air between it and myself.

We stand in the rock field and watch for a moment. The blaze races across the mountain.
We watch the last leg of the trail to Oowah Lake disappear in a rolling cloud of smoke.

The floor falls out beneath me.

That was it. The door is closed. The drawbridge is down, the moat is dry, and an army is charging us from all directions.

I know that it probably isn't the flames that will kill us.

I know that the smoke inhalation will burn our lungs like battery acid.

I know that we will fall unconscious and be cooked.

I know that the fire is less than a mile from us, and closing fast.

I know that it doesn't smell like woodsmoke, but like ash.

I know that this fire stands five stories tall, easily.

I know that the scariest part is the sound.

I clasp her hand.

I know that it sounds like a freight train.

I know that the fire sucks in the air around us, pulling us like blades of grass into the inferno.

I know that the fire wants us.

The last thing I saw before I died wasn't my family, or my memories all at once. It wasn't my friends or any type of failed aspiration. I saw the people who started this illegal campfire. I saw the smoke and the wisps of flame take off while nobody was watching. I saw them drinking from their bottle of water, still full.
I saw the part of me that wanted to give up, wanted to stop and be devoured by this hungry thing.
And I saw myself die.

The rest of me, full to the brim with light, stands holding the hand of a girl brighter than the fires of hydrogen burning on the sun.

This is not where our lives end. This granite field will not be our tomb. We will not be interred on this creosote memorial, smited by the forces of wildfire and ignorance.

Grand County Search & Rescue finally answers the call. Make a run for Medicine Lake. Back, past the evil mine road. Back into the smoke. They have a plane in the air, there is a clear path, but we have to move. Now.

The fire and the nebula of smoke the size of most east coast states towers over us. We run away from it, but the blaze tries to suck us back in. The sound and the fury grips us with wispy claws, we tear back downhill toward Medicine Lake.

The sun drops below the horizon, we are in darkness. We cross Hell Canyon again and sit down on a fire road. The fire rages on the far side of the canyon, swallowing where we were just standing in its entirety.

We get on the phone with SAR again, and ask how long it is going to be. The fire is moving and the temperature is dropping. We ask if we should set up camp. They say no, to wait, but we would later find out that they had interpreted this as us declaring that we were setting up camp. They told the deputy that was looking for us to wait until morning.

We set up our headlamps flashing an SOS signal, unaware that nobody was on their way until morning. Her and I each consume a few thousand more calories and crawl into our compressed sleeping bags. My body is deciding to shut off, whether I'm inside the bag or not.
I awake, some time during the night to the sound of a motor. My headlamp broadcasts red light into the trees.

...---...---...---

Where is that sound coming from?

The fire has laid down. Relative humidity has risen, the fuel is wetter and the wind is calmer. Still, it's burned halfway through the canyon and is inching toward us.

A plane. Plane.

Flying low, instruments of radar and infrared oscillating and scanning and surveying. I grab my light and shine it frantically in the sky. The plane stays its course. What did I want? For it to land and pick us up? I go back to sleep.

The wildfire looks like streams of magma, cracking through the crust.

...

Evacuation comes in the morning.

We made it out alive. A little bit smoked, a little bit frayed, but very much alive.

Still, I know

That a part of me died that day.

After The Fire

After The Fire

"Do not despair; one of the thieves was saved. Do not presume; one of the thieves was damned." Attr. Saint Augustine, *The Repentance of Robert Greene*

It is a 0330 start for me the day after the fire.
See ya later Cam, a Talenti full of overnight oats in the saddlebag of my bicycle.
I ride through the valley without a light. There aren't any cars out this time of day.
Manuel is the breakfast cook at the restaurant here. When he first arrived, he asked me about a giant animal with spikes coming from its head that took a run at him while he rode his bicycle.
This was in October, during the rut.
Convent and Pariott Mesas stand as goliaths, watching the

silence below. A band of stars, the Milky Way, spills across the sky. There is no moon tonight.

I get in the company's sprinter van, which they purchased rather recently.

We use it for tours, but only if we need to. We have other vehicles that can fit fewer folk.

With a turn of the broken key, the alarms start blaring.

CHANGE OIL

BRAKE WEAR--CHANGE BRAKES

SERVICE OVERDUE 6800 MILES

This is normal. It is okay. It has to be. It isn't like I'm putting the lives of these people at risk by driving them around steep drop offs and rocky cliffs all day.

The brakes will hold like they always have.

If we send it to the shop, we have to stop selling tours.

That's how business is done at this place.

Pay the fine, don't buy the permit.

I load up the cooler with ice and get their $5 value, $35 lunches.

Don't worry, they come with a reusable bag that we aren't allowed to reuse.

I collected them from this season. Some more Moab kids have lunchboxes now.

The family is late, as usual.

What's it to them? They only spent $1100 on this 5 hour tour. Lunch was extra. They get free disposable water bottles, though.

As we pull out of the ranch, the headlights spill over Beet going for his morning walk out in the darkness.

He's in the middle of a polyphasic sleep schedule to accommodate for our heat.

The sky lightens.

"Isn't this a sunrise tour?" The guest asks. I suppose he forgot that he was late. They're from New Jersey.

"Yes,"

"Then step on it,"

"It's actually governed," I say. Is that true?

I'm already going 45 in a 45. Brake failure here means a death sentence straight into the river with 10 passengers. It is governed. Governed by me.

The valley opens up to Moab, obscured by smoke.

We get to Arches and pay the fee.

We get to the Windows section, where they disregard the guidelines I've just given them.

It isn't usually the kids I have to stop from screaming and carving,

it is the parent.

And even when it is the child,

It is the parent.

When the child falls silent or falls with tears,

The parents tell them to shut up.

We struggle to park at Delicate Arch, where the asphalt wishes it was just a few degrees hotter to melt the tires.

Disneyland: Arches Adventure. Is it all that different? I couldn't tell you.

It doesn't seem like anyone here can be the cow, doesn't seem like they ever could be.

We get to the 'hairy' section of the trail. If you've been there, you know what I mean. A 5 foot wide walk with a small drop on the side. I've seen strollers pushed over this, but these people need coaching to get across. I'm happy to do so. We came all this way.

Every 13 minutes on average, a water bottle is dropped down the cliff face. I've timed it.

Today, a young man in flip flops runs down to collect them.

There's an arch in the Devil's Garden called Landscape Arch. It is thin, and looks like you could shout loud enough to make it crumble. Behind it is a rock wall.

Through Delicate Arch is supposed to be my Lovely La Sals. A naming mix up switched these two titles, the thin Landscape Arch should be Delicate, and vice versa. They'll tell you this isn't true.

But usually, in an innocent world, you can see the mountains through Delicate. Not today, though. The smoke putrefies and cascades upward into the sky.

I have a running theory. The Standard Index of Campervans.

In both the upper and lower Delicate Arch parking lots, if the total number of camper vans numbers greater than 5, we are still in peak season. We have been in peak season for almost a year now.

Invasion of the camper van.

They speak of their biggest bummer of the year, that they only made it to ski 96 days this year. They, unfortunately, failed to make it to the 100 day club.

They wear brand new shoes, probably #1 on a top 10 list somewhere on the internet, or perhaps whatever was at eye level in the store.

They get blisters because they aren't broken in.

More than once they refuse a path to avoid getting their white trail runners a little bit red from the soil.

Their clothing matches this tune, too. Untried. Untested. By the professionals, sure, it is golden. But these things are new to them, and identify with a way of life that is foreign.

This is how you make acquaintance, and eventually, friend with this landscape.

By all means, buy all means.

That's not how this works.

They're hot, uncomfortable. My thermometer reads 114F. Parents argue, children sweat. Any complaint is met with the sage parental advice to 'stop being a sissy'.

The sagebrush watches, pretending to be indifferent.

I want to comfort them. I ask them about home.

Which one?

The summer one, the winter one, the beach house, or the

Covid project?

We go to Walker Drug and buy beer for their upcoming river trip.

They smile and laugh like the hotel parking lot isn't full of SAR and fire trucks from all over the state. Like there isn't a sign in the store of the fire map, asking for donations for the hungry firefighters, the hotshots. 6,000 today. Jesus.

I want so badly to make these people understand. To make them understand that they should not be upset that they only got to ski 96 days this year.

"Don't you know that I died yesterday? Right there, on that mountain?"

I've tried in the past, to the point that I wanted to leave this town. It seems that folks aren't coming here to appreciate or understand anymore, but to use and abuse.

This isn't a playground.

I've tried, and I keep trying.

Some will even tell you that they understand, that they 'get it'. But, how can you know for sure?

I want them to go through the whole process and to get the most of all this. To be a part of the desert. If they aren't open, that can't work.

You can bring your tourists to the desert, but you can't make them bleed.

Rabbi

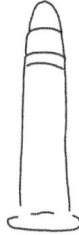

Rabbi

It takes me three days before I manage to do it,
And six missed shots with my .22

I wear the two predecessors like armor.

When it finally happens, it is because I asked.

I now know that when it didn't happen, it is because I did not.

"Please," I said, having missed and scared him once already.

And that was enough.

The funny thing is that there was no bullet hole. Blood dribbled out of his mouth, but the hide was not torn anywhere.

I use him, all of him, for different things.

But there was no bullet hole.

144

The Desert Sentinel

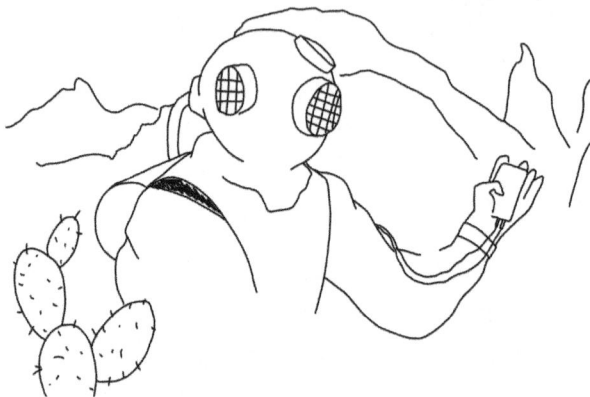

The Desert Sentinel

Water is H2O, hydrogen two parts, oxygen one,
But there is also a third thing, that makes it water
And nobody knows what it is.
-D.H. Lawrence, *"A Third Thing"*

It doesn't rain here.

That's what most people think.

Sometimes I think that, too.

It's a desert, after

all.

When the visitors and the tourists arrive they generally
suffer from faint altitude sickness.

The noses of some bleed.
It's a ritual,   I tell them.
Lay out the red carpet for your arrival.
Pay your tax with your blood.

Increased solar radiation cooks others until they are as red
as the rocks.
Overheats their cell phone beyond usage
Pops tires.

The sharp greasewood and prickly pear swing their wooden
weapons at their calves
More blood still,
Drawn out and filling the mudcrack like the
water we wish would.

The GPS doesn't work without internet,
And the map doesn't work without a mind.
The water--further still.

They purchase and drink the plastic to
Take the edge off.
Sometimes it works.
But if you're thirsty,
It's usually too late.

Here lies Peter, who only drank one liter
That's what Laura and I tell them.
They laugh, but they don't listen.

They travel to Wolfe Ranch
A cabin, a root cellar,

And water.

That's the only reason they made it out here. A small, stink-
ing creek so rife with mineral deposits you'll get a kidney
stone just thinking about it.

And they tried to saddle the bucking Colorado, too. They
tried with a dam that will fail, but did not avoid poison.
It creates Lake Powell, where I used to pilot boats for clients.
The water fights back by leaving. The marinas are closing,
one by one.

What they don't know is that once their bottle is empty
And without resupply,
They'll be dead within 48 hours.
Or perhaps they know, and don't want to think
                            about it.

Deep sea divers.
We tread on
Oceania of prehistory.
Take all you need to survive a few hours. If you're skilled,
maybe even a few days or more.

The tether is strong in this part of the world.
Your Jeep
Your submarine
Your flip-flops
Your flippers
Your lifeline
Your cellphone
Your water

Your air

That tether is all that keeps your heart beating.
And still they don't think. They go on top of the buttes and
mesas
And bust the crust
And go out to god-knows-where-but-Search-And-Rescue-
might-not

It is a simple enough process to avoid this. Asking is the
easy part. Listening is not.

This is not the mission of The Desert Sentinels.

To receive permission
Is to avoid
Trespass.

All this is more delicate than the arch.
More elephantine than the butte.
To not receive permission and to
Be wounded,

Is to face the fact that
Maybe

The desert doesn't want you here.

....

To know your permission is to ask one final time and to
listen
To receive permission is to continue your dive,

To slide behind the veil and have conversations
And
to be versed in the chorus of the rocks

Speak to them
And they will sing for you.

This is how you will be told to be here.

Then, and only then, may you walk on the ocean's floor.
Among the coral reefs of sagebrush and juniper. Watch as
the sea creatures navigate--the chipmunk acting squirrely
among the reeds--the pronghorn leaping over the sediment
bed.

There were parts of history here where
So much liquid
Blocked out the light.

It is the opposite of that now.

The reduction of water-loss pressure on the sandstone
Causes it to rely on internal glues.
Sometimes that glue fails and mounds of entrada
Collapse and obliterate into tiles of shrapnel.
A loud sound, but usually nothing more relevant than that
to our fragile bodies.

There are other ways it tries to kill you. Don't worry.

Two years ago I was terrified in this raging water.
I became trapped, submerged between a capsized raft and a
mound of sandstone
I found and kicked and punched
But the river was stronger than I. The river is always stron-

ger.

And I knew that it wanted to keep me. This cold place was to become my tomb--that much had already been decided.

Stop fighting for a moment, speak.

We shake hands, and I push the raft off

I had baptized others in this river many times before.

Catholics, baptists, even some Christians.

With my mouth open as a baby bird's breaking through the surface to suck in pneumonic life

That's when I knew. This priest had lustrated me.
 by volition of its own.

It doesn't happen often, but it does happen

And usually much less violently

To be pushed to the brink by the land and the water is a rite of tribulation.
To survive this is to push onto the final stage.

Two others I know have made it this far.
Beet and Cam.

But the title is not yet granted.

…

Water falls from the sky in droplets. This does not mean

that it is raining.

Your heartbeat quickens. The flora opens. It smells like rain.

The sandstone beneath your feet is dotted with dark circles,
An image developing.
Dark clouds roll across the sky. It looks like rain.

To watch and to feel and to know
Is the discipline of the Sentinels

It will not rain today.

Water cascades in sheets, a tapestry pirouetting toward the
sand.
The heat cooks it, turning to steam before it hits the ground.
It evaporates, pulling skyward in a U. Water meets water on
the endless roundabout of the Cumulonimbus Superhigh-
way.

It has not rained in over two months.

This is heartbreak, materialized.
The land needs it.
Your spirit needs it.
Problems and toxins
That weigh way down

Down here,
they all wash out in the rain.

Yet, some do not seek this. Some seek to challenge and to conquer. This is okay with the right conversations.

Some try to cross the river,
Insisting that their muscles provide more
 security
than
Any PFD could provide.

Some think that they are fast enough
To
outrun the sun

Some are not as intuitive or as intentional as The Sentinels.
These traits are gifts of
the sun
the sand
the rocks
and the trees.

These tribulations humble those that partake.
They begin the conversation,
The handshake

You watch.
You feel.

The final leap is to know.

The Sentinels watch this rain defy gravity.
And they watch the professional swimmer deflate

The conversation reaches their ears. The rocks and the river
speak.

And The Sentinel then knows
That
No matter how choked
The rain will come
And

Some will tell you that you can fight the water.
And they are not wrong.
You can fight,
but

The river always wins.

CISCO

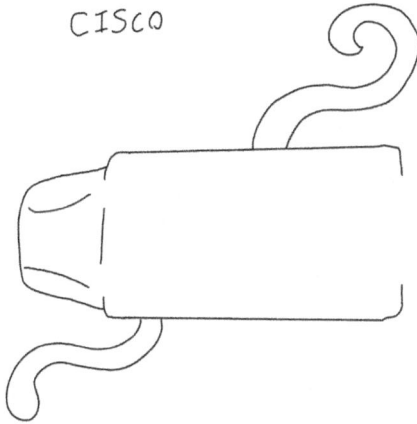

Cisco

"Water, water, water....There is no shortage of water in the desert but exactly the right amount, a perfect ratio of water to rock, water to sand, insuring that wide free open, generous spacing among plants and animals, homes and towns and cities, which makes the arid West so different from any other part of the nation. There is no lack of water here unless you try to establish a city where no city should be."
Edward Abbey, *Desert Solitaire: A Season in the Wilderness*

I follow Marlow's advice and find myself driving out from the ranch I work on to Cisco. I have driven by the town quite a few times, but only stopped at Cisco Landing, the takeout for most Westwater trips.

I go while the sun is still up on a hot August day. The sky is virtually cloudless, save one massive mushroom shaped cloud pressing into the stratosphere.

The road from Moab comes to a T. Turn left to get to I-70 faster, turn right to take the Cisco bypass road, the right way. It is a straight track of old asphalt that putters through an open expanse of desert from here until Fruita. This used to be the main highway, until they built the interstate.

It isn't more than a few minutes before I'm in town. I would estimate that roughly ⅔ of the buildings here have been reduced to rubble or are about to be. I pull up into the gravel lot and pass three "we're open" signs. The shop is made of wood, and is well kept and clean on the outside. Statues line the property as my boot heels melt onto the rock. A giant gorilla, vultures as gargoyles, and a mermaid riding a bicycle. A sign above the door reads "Buzzards Belly General Store". The door opens easily and a wave of cold air hits me. The floorboard creeks beneath my weight. A woman stands behind the counter, a man on the other side. They look at me.

"Howdy, what can I help you with?" The woman asks.

"Howdy, would you happen to know where I could find Eileen?" I ask. The man and woman look at each other, then back at me.

"She's not here anymore," the woman says. I purse my lips and think for a moment. All that excitement for this? How could Marlow not know that she was dead? I suppose he wouldn't have ridden his bike out here, but,

"Is she…?"

"What I mean is that she's in Colorado,"

"Oh," I smile, and we share a short laugh. "I'm a friend of Marlow's, he told me to come and ask for the ten cent tour from Eileen."

"Oh, that I can help you with. I'm not her but I know her, I'm Jean,"

"Just slap your dime on the table and take a walk for yourself." The man says, wearing mostly denim.

Behind the woman is a sign with a gun barrel pointed at the reader. It says "there's nothing in this store worth dying for". She's got a pistol on her hip, some kind of Glock probably with a green polymer handle. The weapon nests in a beautifully ornate leather holster that is likely worth more than most cowboy boots.

With their blessing, I walk around the seemingly deserted town. Not a tree--not even a shrub in sight. Just tan, gravelly desert. What buildings still stand are covered in eye popping colors and display more personality and wit than an entire neighborhood's worth of tract housing. Exploring ghost towns is a hobby of mine, and I've seen a great deal of them. Although I would later discover that the population of Cisco was somewhere between 5 and 6, it became rapidly clear that this town had something most of the others did not. As I walk the main drag, a pulse echoes from around me. Inaudible. This town has a heartbeat, and this town is alive.

Before me stands three giant, rusted pipes tied together with a chain at the top. A rope dangles down in the center with a disk of wood on the end. A burning hot rope swing would be wonderful, but I am a visitor here and I do not risk it. Next to this is a teepee made of smaller sections of the same rusted piping, with angled wooden boards forming the outer walls in a lovely cascade. Inside it is paved with broken slabs of marble countertop, a single anti-slip kitchen mat in the center.

Nearby is the rusted hood of an antique car, propped against a house. On it is delicately and artfully portrayed a detailed map of the entire city, which boasts short descriptions of the buildings that are still standing and those that have collapsed. This map tips me off to a few locations that I otherwise may have missed. A nearby bus is painted in pale blue and golden cream-sheep ascending a peak on one side. The other side displays two revolvers firing at one another and creating a cloud of gunsmoke.

Further into town the body of a well loved red pickup sleeps. It's still got snow chains on the tires, and a home-made bed cap that extends well over the cabin. Tucked into the siding like shingles are a few hundred La Croix cans. The tops and bottoms are removed, leaving just the sheet of metal that was then flattened by the artist.

A pearly white antique and rounded Crosley refrigerator stands watch outside another building. The metal logo hangs on its side. A washer/dryer combo is nearby, the washer in the bottom stuffed full of rock and sand. The dryer on top asks for a donation on Venmo @HomeOfT-heBrave, with a well done, hand painted design. It says that every bit helps. Anything to help keep this place beating.

Eileen's name is all over this place. It's like I got here just as she left home. Her website is written on a sign, on the web-page it details the mission of this painted place.

"Home of the Brave is an artist-in-residence program based in Cisco, Utah. Reimagined by visual artist Eileen Muza, the former ghost town is now a working embodiment of the values that she and others in the extended Cisco family have worked to foster: artistic freedom, creative repurposing, social inclusivity and sustainable growth.
Home of the Brave is committed to cultivating a space where artists of any medium, means, or self-identification, can immerse themselves and create freely amidst the beauty

and solitude of the high desert."

This place, I think, is most of the beauty in this part of the desert. It is abundantly clear to me now that unlike Jackass Joe's, this place is not occupied by aliens, lizard-reptilian overlords, or artists.

It is occupied by the Desert Sentinels.

I'm visiting another station, I suppose.

Next to the massive town sign revealing that we are, in fact, in The Home of the Brave Art Residency is a pole. The top of the pole has four arrows pointing to the center of town, each with a word on them. Together they read "Oh no! You're in Cisco! Utah"

Centerpieces here are subjective. Mine was the giant bus. The outside is painted cleanly with a woman in a jumpsuit with a dog. She wears painting equipment, the dog looks like it has spotted a cottontail. The jumpsuit is embroidered with the word "Muza", while the dog wears a bandana embroidered with "Rema".

Rema and Muza, standing watch.

Somehow equally impressive to this painting is a massive snake made of wood and stone coiling around and penetrating through the bus. I can't wrap my mind around the snake, it is as thick as an oil drum and looks petrified, like I'd better not get too close to it.

I explore the rest of the town, dropping into the cellars of collapsed homes and scrambling back out onto the scorching earth. I am told that the wind here causes these structures to collapse, hence why so many have underground sections. This is uncommon in this region. The majority of the buildings are made of old railroad ties and spikes, which have now buckled under the pressure of the soil.

I walk to the old airstrip that was denoted on the map, which now seems to only be a slightly flatter piece of rectangular land. Perhaps that's all it ever was.

The oil derrick, as noted, wasn't more than a mystifying

depression in the ground. Olive? Canola? I'm hungry.
I tread onward, the heat baking me like the potato that I am.
The thermometer in my kit reads 117F.
My final stop in this end of town is the old gas station.
Inside is more broken glass and a collection of posters on
the wall of the collapsing place. Sunlight streams in through
what little roof is left and casts long, bright beams on the
images of a rock band. There's another photo of a man with
large glasses holding a machete, and a black and white
image next to that of a woman brandishing a sickle. Below
these is a confusing sight, a baby doll next to a bottle of
booze and missing a leg. Don't worry too much, though, as
the leg is still there. It just isn't attached.

   The remainder of images in this place are of folks
having a grand time together, sharing sweaty smiles inside
a building. Maybe it was this gas station. Probably not. No
pumps are left outside, but an overturned cement block is.
It is as long and wide as a trough, and has detailed spray
painting across it, and it faces the road. On the left side is a
woman in a motorcycle helmet with an X painted over her.
On the right side is a cowboy aiming a rifle, also with an X.
In the center, in large orange letters reads "THE DIREC-
TIVE". Above this reads "No more masters".
The green writing in the center reminds me where I am.
It reads "The Vanishing Point". I drive through here with
clients often. I tell them that this span of the earth is the
highest concentration of alien abductions in the U.S. Is that
true? I have no idea. Probably not.
Even if it were true, I'm not sure you'd be able to trust the
institution that gave you such a statistic.
I know the sign at the Residency listed Utah, but I'm not so
sure about that. I could have looked the location of Cisco
up, but I intentionally did not. It is not something that one
should find on a GPS. Cisco may be close to the border of
Colorado, but in my opinion it doesn't exist in either state. It

may not even be on this continent or planet, for all I know. But what I do know is that this place is beyond normal, and beyond special.

Jean and I became friends, and I try to stop by when I find myself heading to Junction or Palisade for some peaches. She tells me that there's no running water in the whole town. I made a note to bring her some water from Matrimony Springs, where many have found themselves to be wed to the land.

She tells me a final thing before I leave. She tells me that her favorite thing about this place is the stars. I ask her if she has a favorite constellation, and she says that she doesn't know many.

I used to think that you cannot love something until you know it. With her words, now I'm not so sure.

Sheets of Green

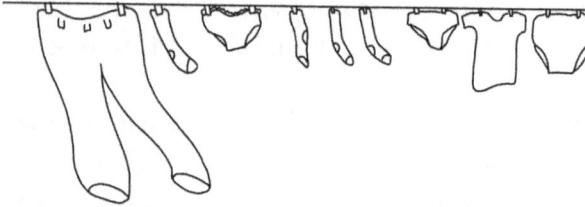

Sheets of Green
1.
When I lived in the mountains,
I thought the same color meant the same taste.
Tangerines, oranges and the sun. Citrus.
When I saw my great-grandmother peel a tangerine with her bare hands
while men used knives for oranges, she became God.
I imagined what she could do with the sun.
-JP Infante, Yasica, Puerto Plata

Cam peels an old orange for me in the passenger seat while I drive her Subaru Outback. A light rain pecks at the windshield as we bound up and down the green hills outside of Durango, Colorado. She puts a slice into my mouth and puts the pieces of the peel in the small depression near the door handle. Knowing her, they'll stay there until they dry up and become as brittle as crackers.
When I was at the riots in Washington, D.C. I carried a bread bag full of fruit and vegetable scraps. It was a hard place with streets full of battered, bloody and screaming and

defeated faces. This mobile compost bag confused many, but delighted most. The depression in the car next to the door handle is a high speed mobile composting center. We once discussed filling a glovebox with worms and soil for more rapid digestion, but ultimately decided that if a head-on collision were to occur it would severely confuse the first responders. We decided that it would save the gravedigger precisely one spadeful. The mobile composting center is ingenious and indicative of her out of the box problem solving skills. I like this about her.

She is a citrus girl in more ways than one. She peels another orange, dark red on the inside and quite old. She says we accidentally got a blood orange somehow, which I had never had. It was bitter and tasted like a salted lime mixed with DEET. I was hungry. She kept peeling, and we laughed as we took turns eating it. This was a sheet of green.

In the backyard of my childhood home, my mother and I would dig a hole and fill it with water. The result was a pool of chocolate colored mud. The treehouse above us hid us in a spot of shade. A summer delight. My hands were cool inside the pit. We took the Star Wars action figures that my brother didn't play with any more and made them fight and swim and mine and crawl through the mud. Over a decade later I would borrow an electric saw and begin tearing down the rotted, collapsing treehouse to build a wall inside my mom's garage. I only sliced through a few beams (and nearly my leg) before John, the owner of the saw, came to help me. Together we took down the treehouse. The last thing we did was pull the wooden 4x4 beam out of the ground. It was covered in an emerald colored moss, the wood saturated and permeated by many seasons in the northeast. We pulled the deeply set beam out by grabbing near the top for leverage. When it finally gave, it uprooted like a tree. In a way, I suppose it was a tree. In the crater that remained, an arm stuck out. Not a human one, and not an animal's either.

A tiny plastic arm that was thinner than the width of my pinky. The Jedi, Luke Skywalker, had been entombed in the soil for over 13 years before this unsolicited exhumation. I pulled him out and washed him off with the hose like we used to. Sometimes the sheets of green are buried and forgotten.

Cam is a park ranger in Arches National Park. We get up before the sun and french press coffee together. I don't like coffee, but I like her. We eat scrambled eggs and drink the hot coffee while watching the sun bake the rocks into glowing coals at her cabin. The iron in the rocks causes them to be red, but this is a sheet of green.

After my father left, we chased one another with inflatable Incredible Hulk hammers outside. I executed the ultimate move: I climbed under the orangey plastic safety fence. I knew he couldn't follow and so, by forfeit, I had won our battle. I wasn't wearing a jacket, even though he told me I ought to. The ground was frozen and the trees were barren. Sandy The Golden Retriever ran about. All of this was brown. But it was green, too.

Cam and I dance at the locals beach on the banks of the manmade Lake Powell. The solar oven roasting sweet potatoes nearby. The water level was at a record low, which is a phrase that will hopefully be repeated often and indefinitely. We swing dance with hoops and spins and dips, this is a sheet of green.

As a young scout, my close friend Jack and I learned to sail in the warm waters of the Chesapeake Bay. One day, the wind changed direction and the boom nailed me square in the nose, sending me backward and into the water like a scuba diver who suddenly got sent to their surprise party. We stand on the coast hours later, doing a leg sweep maneuver to find the glasses that had been knocked from my face. This was the first practical application of a SAR technique in my life. We gave up after a few minutes of this and opted to instead jump around in the waters. Across the bay was Fort Aberdeen, a military proving ground for experimental ordinance (complete with an on site Tim Horton's). Every few minutes, as soon as you let your guard down, a detonation would come from the fort. You'd hear the singular, thundering blast first. Then feel the slap in the air. Then, after a few more seconds, the shockwave would reach you through the water. A concussive cannon that signaled the death of another tribute. This was also a sheet of green.

A flood in Poultney, Vermont once covered one of my favorite trails in three feet of water at the conclusion of spring. Twigs, branches, and entire trees including their leaves floated in the turquoise brown water. To swim there was to literally swim among sheets of green.

In Michigan, I wear a full suit of camouflage and cover myself in mud. With an accomplice, Abby, we cover a dead tree in the lake with grapevine leaves and place trash nearby. We wait for Cam to approach so I can jump out and scare her. In the meantime, I nest in sheets of green.

I climb with Jake at Cinema and Theater, a massive wall of sandstone across from Takeout Beach in Moab. I'm belaying him from the ground, the rope goes from a pile on the ground, through the ATC at my pelvis, up to the anchor and down to Jake, who is the counterweight on the other end. He's got to be at least 40 feet above me, hanging on an overhang. If I were to fail to catch him, he wouldn't hit me, but would instead continue another 80 feet to the jagged, micah rich sandstone below. If he slips, he won't fall that far. That's why I'm here. The friction of the rope through my ATC, with the rope pulled to my hip, will stop that from happening.

"Shiii-FALLING!" He shouts. I lock the rope immediately. I drop down to a crouch to avoid launching from the weight drop on the other side of the rope. Something in the sand-stone ledge shifts internally. The rock I am standing on gives way and I slip, executing a perfect flying kick out into the troposphere. In the panic, I lose a few more feet of rope and clutch--for our lives--locking the rope in the ATC as we swing freely over the 80 foot drop. All this within a second. It seems that the world's longest seconds happen when they might be your last.

"Do not let go of the rope." he says.
"Why would I let go of the rope?" I ask. No safety knot.

I'm wearing a helmet. Jake isn't. It wouldn't matter anyway. Not at this height. No bought adoubt it.

We kick back and forth, increasing our momentum on the world's most fun impromptu rope swing. I'm still wearing my climbing shoes, and manage to heel hook around a boulder to pull us in.

Exhilarating. Another sheet of green.

A few months later, Cam and I began a rappel down a lower section of rock that was only a 50 foot drop, but at a route just adjacent to the previous incident. Still high enough to be a near guaranteed death sentence. The rappel involved locking into the anchors, which were on the side of the cliff. A crawl on your stomach to hook in. Then, the challenging part. The chains, combined with the padding of the rope, meant that once you went over the edge you faced a 3 foot drop. During that drop, your fate was unknown. You could fall the remaining 47, or stop at 3 and complete with a controlled descent. I had done this once before, in January with Manuel and Jake when a snowstorm hit us mid-climb.

I clung to the rock, wishing to be absorbed into it. I slid down the face and stopped with a jolt at the 3 foot mark, but I had ripped my skin, my shirt, and my pants in the process. My fist was pressed against the bright red sandstone, every knuckle torn open and quickly bleeding, leaving a trail down my forearm and dropping to the depth below. Iron to iron. Rust to dust.

This, too, was a sheet of green.

I lived out of a 1966 Roadrunner travel trailer in the La Sal mountains with my pitbull, Kai. Around the same time every night, my cellphone would go off.
When we first arrived in the mountains, Kai was nearly one year old. He saw his first cow from the back seat of my F.O.R.D. Found On Road Dead/Fix Or Repair Daily. The Ford explorer. The Ford exploder. That truck would later die in Glenwood Springs, Colorado. It got melted down into walkers and support equipment for the children's hospital in Denver.
When Kai saw this first cow, he went ballistic. "How come this dog is so big?"

Mmmmmm was the vibration of my phone. Kai seemed particularly interested in it. We ate dinner together each night in the wildflower field.

The peculiar thing was that I never received a message when this alert would go off. I didn't even have service.

Impossible.

Mmmmmmmm. Once again. Twice in the same night? This couldn't be. I hold the phone and stand silently. The vibration sound again, but my phone doesn't vibrate. We go outside.

There, twenty feet away, stands the first cow that Kai ever saw. It took her two months, but she finally tracked us down near Mt. Tuk. She moos softly, but with intent. Mmmmmm.

She turned and ran through the scrub oak, Kai and I gave chase. She was so fast that we lost her after a minute or so of pursuit through thick foliage, but she led us to a thick, bright green tract of woodland. Kai and I run as fast as we can together, dodging branches and rabbits and cow pies. This was a sheet of green.

The first sheet that Cam and I experienced together came in the form of Jif Natural peanut butter plummeting from the sky and nailing me square on the shoulder.

I was hiking Old Mandolin Canyon alone. There was one other car in the lot.

"Hello? Is there someone up there?" I called to the ledge above me. The trail diverged about a mile back, with two pathways you could take, an upper and a lower. There was no answer.

I finished my hike, just a few more miles as an out and back. When I returned to the parking lot the other car, a Subaru Outback, was still there. I decided to sit in the last rays of the rapidly retreating winter sun and wait a moment.

A young woman with a knowing smile walked out of the trail. I produced the peanut butter.

"Did you...happen to throw this at me?" I asked.

She hadn't. However, the banana she ate with it had preoc-
cupied her mind to the point that she accidentally knocked
it over, where it quickly rolled off the cliff and hit me. She
heard my "ow", but thought it better not to reply when I
called up to her. And here I was, just hoping that peanut
butter falling from the sky was to be a regular occurrence
from here on out.

We exchanged phone numbers.

Some time and a lot of love later, we run around a lake in
northern Michigan.
A downpour has just begun, hurling cold rain down on
our bare shoulders. We run in sandals uphill, downhill,
whatever. Through puddles and overgrown branches across
the trail. Thunder cracks across the sky. We are drenched,
completely soaked. My worries and fears that were born in
the desert are gone as we fly through the forest together.
It is true what they say; it will all wash out in the rain. The
land and stories I love are made of sheets of green, and this
warrior wraps me in them.

Destabilization Factors of Human and Coyote Communities In Relation To Climate Change

Vigil

"Be humble, for you are made of earth. Be noble, for you are made of stars."
-Serbian proverb

Sandstone and granite chunks beneath my boots.

An improbable meeting, just as ours.

My fire burns quietly, composed in small flames and bright coals.
Reflection of a mind on vigil.

The pines tower around me,
Long and dancing shadows cast into the night.

They whisper.

Purple and white heat lightning illuminates the valley.

I came here to kill you. You knew this.

I've been out here for seven days.

Walking the salt mountains in search. I found the signs of you,
but not the thing in actuality.

I know that you found me. I know that you watch me while I sleep.

So tonight I do not; I'll wait for you.

A conversation is two people.

I hold a vigil.

This spring water that flows from the earth, a gift of sanctuary and respite. This is my wine.

These currants and elderberries
Cover my fingers with pungent ink.
This is your blood.

This dandelion stands vibrant against the underwater blue of the night. It is bitter and unsprayed. This is my bread.

The western screech owl is somewhere out there. They speak, filling the crisp atmosphere with song. This is our sermon.

These mossy, saturated logs covered with shelf mushrooms and lichen, they provide a bridge across water, and a wet seat after a long day. These are the pews.

The pine needles smolder on the edge of the rocks. This is the incense, filling the air with a sappy, familiar aroma. It smells like this, like my home.

Above us, thousands of pinpricks dot across the sky. The Milky Way spills in a celestial ribbon. They watch, silent and sure. This is our congregation.

I fast for you,
I kneel and I pray for you.

This is my church.

This is where you and I meet, in The Cathedral of the Pines.

Step out.

I hear you walking, but I would not have if I weren't listening.

                    Step out.

The weapon of the 21st century predator is in my hands. I know I won't use it.

                    Step up.

That is why I came here, but that is not why I stay. I lay down the weapon.

Step forward.

You do, toward me. I bow and lower to my knees. Your eyes, balls of white fire burning hotter than the one behind me.

More than a reflection?
Step in.

You don't come any closer. We can't hear one another at this distance. That's for the best. We speak without words. You don't speak English, and I don't speak coyote.

Years later, a child will ask me how many are hearing this sermon, how many are in the congregation.

You know this number. You have it memorized, although it changes with the setting of each sun.

You know so much that I could never conceive of.

The 21st century predator is in this holy place. He makes eye contact with the other, and converses.

I look at the one true Desert Sentinel.

I know that because I reach,

I know,
That I am the best embodiment that I can be.

An embodiment and The Sentinel, I see that now for what it is. He instructs me to wear the armor of the three who came before.
And
Of the fire.
This is what makes you the One.

I am here
       I am here
              I am here

The priest speaks to me,
 Here,
 in The Cathedral of the Pines.

Outrun The Sun

Epilogue: Outrun the Sun

Clouds in the sky, the pressure drops. They're not the white ones that adorn our days like ribbons. No, these are heavy with promise of respite. This is for us. This is for those who do not try to outrun the sun, but wait on the prayer of the rain.

The wind rips bugscreens from windows, tarps from cars, and yanks bottles off of tables to shatter on the rocks. The knocks travel from cabin to cabin. It is time. Finally.

Beet is out at once, barefoot and in a kilt. Mike Hawk is here, too. We make a run for the field. The electrical fence works on a cyclical current, we'll be fine. Probably.

A minefield of goatheads, cow pies, and horse apples. We stand and watch the low cloud swallow Fisher Towers, the Titan, then Convent Mesa. It is here, and it is good. The sky opens up, dumping tens of thousands of gallons of water on our eager, greasy hair. We hoot and holler, jump and slide and drink and shout and love.

Sometimes living on this planet feels like a state of mourning, but there is still work to be done. We cannot rest yet.

Perhaps this whole book is a nice way of me saying 'get the hell off my lawn'.
Although you pay taxes on it, this isn't your land. And you know what? It isn't mine, either. This is everyone's land. But above all else, it is nobody's land, and it never was.

Sun baked and sandal tanned toes dig into the softening, fragrant earth as we run through the cascades of water, falling in curtains down from heaven. This is our gift. This is a sheet of green.

Moab is home to a unique sport: waterfall hunting. The downpour, moving quickly so as to avoid absorption in the porous sandstone, rockets off of cliff edges in spectacular displays of color and magnificence. The cottonwoods sing, sending their children unto the wind to find sanctuary. The crypto swells and smiles.

Waterfalls dropping torrents of liquid pour over everything, petroglyphs, bones, and rock. The red streams pound over the black asphalt and cut off traffic, not even headlights will make it through this. The veins of this world bleed into the Colorado River, turning her rust red with fresh blood.

My name is on the front of this book, but I did not get here alone. To say so could not be further from the actual truth of the matter. So many people helped me get to where I am today, from teaching me how to be outside all the way to helping me edit this book. I'd love to thank each and every one of you, but there simply isn't space. The names below will have to do, for now.
Thank you,

Emma Anderberg, for trading places with me, for making killer coffee, and for having two of the greatest dogs I have ever met (NOT Jerry).

Emma Oley, for being a constant friend since we were kids, for editing this book, for being one of the most intelligent people I know, and for always being willing to look at the weird things I make.

Beet Turnipseed, who thinks that Mike is actually George W. Hayduke's long lost grandson. Thank you for long, late night conversations over fires and trails and for being a spiritual leader to me. And thanks for editing this mess, too.

Cam, for daring to lead, for calling me out, and for pushing me so that we can be uncomfortable together--that's where the growth happens. As much as I hate to admit it, a big reason this project came to fruition is because I wanted to impress you. That still counts, right? Thank you for always being by my side and tuning into our world with me. Thank you, also, for editing this book. They say that mycelium connects all living things. I think that you do, too.

Jamie Williams, for the endless enamoring conversations about overalls and plants. When someone asks me in green and white 'Who's Your Farmer?', I can proudly say your name.

Ray Walker, for helping me accomplish odd jobs and build strange contraptions with precisely the wrong tools and materials.

Doc, for providing kindness and insight, and for letting me borrow your food processor for not less than six consecutive months, which produced the hummus that powered much of this endeavor.

Luis, for being a constant friend and for being one of the people who genuinely ask how I am doing, and for being the best architect there is.

Laura Sanders, A.K.A. Mountain Rainshadow, for forwarding my mail, for being a steward of our land and for inspiring me to find peace and grace in all that surrounds us.

Monty, for always bringing too many snacks, for experimenting with your coffee, being a reliable dive partner, making amazing curry, and for letting me crash land at your place when I need to.

Jessa, my sister, for checking in and keeping an open mind about all things, and for keeping everything and everyone together. You inspire me.

Manuel, for being the comic relief in all situations, knowing 100 ways to cook an egg, and for reminding me that no matter how challenging the climbing route, all we had to do was to 'just go up'.

Evan, for reminding me constantly that the German race is superior, for carrying a matching skeleton around, for being the best of friends, for always being eager to help with all things, and for hosting me, wherever we may be in the world.

The Hadley's, all of you, for keeping me outside and for encouraging me to grow. And, for telling me to 'Get out, and stay out'. These are some of the best instructions I have ever received.

Mr. Freeman, for teaching me how to write and to always challenge ideas, no matter the source.

Ms. Nowak, for making me fall in love with the world of words.

Fudge, with nuts, for being an objective and grounding figure that is somehow constantly above the storm, and for teaching me how to canyoneer and pushing me to do things that invoke fear.

My parents, for many things that I cannot say here. Most of all, for encouraging me to be me, and being willing to learn together that such a thing is okay.

The Utah Department of Natural Resources, for providing an abundance of literature and doing the very best you can to educate, protect, and provide. You rock.

Mac, for teaching me how to carve and for providing the weapon of the 21st century predator. I'll see you soon.

Becky, for teaching me how to use computers and always being ready to talk about story structure and graphic design.

Marlow, for being the raddest troglodyte I know, for sending me on side quests, for being a traveler in a world of tourists, and for providing essential stories to an ill-traveled world.

Gina, for being the spokesperson of hospitality in the dry, dry desert, for inviting me in, and for teaching me what you know.

Eileen, for bringing color to the brown patch, and for inspiring everyone to create.

The Baker's, for hosting me, for challenging my ideas, and for providing the harness that holds the field glasses I use to watch coyotes, and the spray I use to keep bears at bay.

Ron Thomas, for being a reliable friend and the most helpful, quintessential Moab Local anyone could dream of. For long mystery sessions staring at maps and telling the stories of old, the stories of those who came before.

Mike, for teaching me so much, for pulling me out of the mud and out of wildfires (both local and in California. Yeah, it has happened more than once). For helping me make explosives (not connected to the previous fact), for being my reliable transportation into the bush, for being the most loyal friend someone could ask for, and for pretending to humor the idea when I tell you that you should really stop smoking.

The mountains, the desert, and the sandstone sea, for being you.
I am completely
Unequivocally
in love.

The forest is the church,
The pines are the steeple,
This is my crew,
These are my people.

Cedar G. Elkheart is a guide and wilderness first responder in Moab, Utah and uses he/him pronouns. He has a bachelor's degree in Wildlife Conservation and a bachelor's in Sustainable Community Development with an emphasis in Sustainable Food Systems. He also has a master's degree in Ecology, and is an ordained minister in the Four Corners Region. For more content, please visit his website at noceilingpath.square.site, or No Ceiling on Youtube, and check out other written content from the author. Cedar is originally from the Northeast of the United States, and has enjoyed living in more states than he has fingers. He currently lives out of a Honda CR-V that smells like paulo santo, where he wrote this book from the open hatchback overlooking our beloved canyon country.

Miklósi, Adam (4 December 2008). Dog Behaviour, Evolution, and Cognition. Oxford University Press. p. 205. ISBN 9780191580130. Some dogs lead a relatively free life despite being socialized to some extent. These dogs have or can establish a social relation with human(s) and may be fed and sheltered regularly (stray dogs, village dogs).

U.S. Department of Transportation Federal Highway Administration, Wildlands CPR, Wildlife Crossings Toolkit (www.wildlifecrossings.info/beta2.htm), National Park Service, New Mexico Department of Game and Fish, Defenders of Wildlife, U.S. Humane Society

Cell Reports, Parker et al.: "Genomic Analyses Reveal the Influence of Geographic Origin, Migration, and Hybridization on Modern Dog Breed Development" www.cell.com/cell-reports/full … 2211-1247(17)30456-4 , DOI: 10.1016/j.celrep.2017.03.079

Morbidity-mortality factors and survival of an urban coyote population in Arizona, M Grinder and PR Krausmanm, Journal of Wildlife Diseases, jwildlifedis April 1, 2001 vol. 37 no. 2312-317
Johnson, Norman. "Faculty Opinions Recommendation of Genomic Analyses Reveal the Influence of Geographic Origin, Migration, and Hybridization on Modern Dog Breed Development." Faculty Opinions – Post-Publication Peer Review of the Biomedical Literature, 2017, doi:10.3410/f.727547314.793538816.
Poliquin, Melanie /. "Coyote (*Canis latrans*) – Ecological Profile – Section 63." Human & Wildlife Ecology, 12 Apr. 2018, humanwildlifeecology.wordpress.com/2018/02/14/coyote-canis-latrans-ecological-profile-section-63/.

"Ministry of Agriculture, Food and Rural Affairs." How to Differentiate Between Coyote and Dog Predation on Sheep, www.omafra.gov.on.ca/english/livestock/sheep/facts/coy-dog2.htm.

Unep-Wcmc. "WOOD BUFFALO NATIONAL PARK." World Heritage Datasheet, 22 May 2017, www.yichuans.me/datasheet/output/site/wood-buffalo-national-park/.

"Wild Animals." Centers for Disease Control and Prevention, Centers for Disease Control and Prevention, 6 Apr. 2020, www.cdc.gov/rabies/location/usa/surveillance/wild_animals.html.

O'LEARY, ZINA. ESSENTIAL GUIDE TO DOING YOUR RESEARCH PROJECT. SAGE PUBLICATIONS, 2021.

Ray, Barbara. "How High Can a Coyote Jump?" Dublin Ohio USA, 6 Mar. 2020, dublinohiousa.gov/nature/how-high-can-a-coyote-jump/.

Preventing Coyote Conflicts - the Humane Society of the ... www.humanesociety.org/sites/default/files/docs/preventing-coyote-conflicts.pdf.

Aguirre-Sacasa, Roberto, et al. The Crucible. Archie Comic Publications, Inc., 2016.

Audubon, John James, and Daniel Patterson. The Missouri River Journals of John James Audubon. University of Nebraska Press, 2016.

Audubon, John James, and Ben Forkner. Selected Journals and Other Writings. Penguin Books, 1996.

Mather, Cotton, et al. The Wonders of the INVISIBLE World: Observations as Well Historical AS THEOLOGICAL, upon the Nature, the Number, and the Operations of the Devils 1693. Zea Books, 2011.

Coleman, Jon T. Vicious: Wolves and Men in America. New Haven, Connecticut: Yale University Press, 2004.

Hampton, Bruce. The Great American Wolf. New York: Henry Holt and Company, Inc., 1997.

Robinson, Michael J. Predatory Bureaucracy: The Extermination of Wolves and the Transformation of the West. University Press of Colorado, 2005.

Schullery, Paul. The Yellowstone Wolf: A Guide & Sourcebook. Worland, Wymoning: High Plains Publishing Company, Inc., 1996.

Little Jr., Elbert L. (1976). "Map 75, Fraxinus anomala". Atlas of United States Trees. 3 (Minor Western Hardwoods). US Government Printing Office. LCCN 79-653298. OCLC 4053799.

Biota of North America Program, Fraxinus anomala Williams, David B., et al. A Naturalist's Guide to Canyon Country: Falcon GUIDES SERIES. Falcon Guides, 2020. National Parks Service, U.S. Department of the Interior, irma.nps.gov/STATS/Reports/Park/ARCH.

Warren, S.D.; St. Clair, L.L.; Johansen, J.R.; [et al.]. 2015. Biological soil crust response to late season prescribed fire in a Great Basin juniper woodland. Rangeland Ecology and Management. 68(3): 241–247

Warren, S.D. 2014. Role of biological soil crusts in desert hydrology and geomorphology: Implications for military training operations. Reviews in Engineering Geology. 22: 177–186.

Belnap, J.; Warren, S.D. 2002. Patton's tank tracks in the Mojave Desert, USA: An ecological legacy. Arid Land Research and Management. 16: 245–258.

Warren, S.D.; Eldridge, D.J. 2001. Biological soil crusts and livestock in arid ecosystems: Are they compatible? In: Belnap, J.; O.L. Lange, O.L., eds. Biological soil crusts: Structure, function, and management. Berlin, Germany: Springer-Verlag: 403–417.

Belnap, J.; Kaltenecker, J.H.; Rosentreter, R.; [et al.]. 2001. Biological soil crusts: Ecology and management. Technical Reference 1730-2. Denver, CO: U. S. Department of the Interior, Bureau of Land Management. 118 p.

Graves, Will (2007). Wolves in Russia: Anxiety throughout

the ages. Detselig Enterprises. ISBN 978-1-55059-332-7.

Ridler, Keith. "Bill to Kill up to 90% of Idaho Wolves Signed by Governor." AP NEWS, Associated Press, 7 May 2021, ap-news.com/article/us-news-idaho-lifestyle-wolves-bills-f83c-d2449975c977d167c0509bccab24.

"Animals and Animal Products:Dairy." Publication | Cattle Death Loss | ID: vh53wv75j | USDA Economics, Statistics and Market Information System, usda.library.cornell.edu/concern/publications/vh53wv75j.

Peek, Simon F., et al. "Infectious Diseases of the Gastro-intestinal Tract." Rebhun's Diseases of Dairy Cattle, U.S. National Library of Medicine, 2018, www.ncbi.nlm.nih.gov/pmc/articles/PMC7152230/.

Boeckel, Thomas P. Van, et al. "Global Trends in Antimi-crobial Use in Food Animals." PNAS, National Academy of Sciences, 5 May 2015, www.pnas.org/content/112/18/5649.

"The Effects of Antibiotic Use in Animals on Human Health and the Drug Resistance Crisis." Medical News Today, MediLexicon International, www.medicalnewstoday.com/articles/323639.

Dutton, Heidi, et al. "Antibiotic Exposure and Risk of Weight Gain and Obesity: Protocol for a Systematic Re-view." Systematic Reviews, BioMed Central, 24 Aug. 2017, www.ncbi.nlm.nih.gov/pmc/articles/PMC5571496/.

Cooling and Climate Change | Unep - Un Environment Programme. www.unep.org/resources/factsheet/cooling-and-climate-change.

"Climate Change Indicators and Impacts Worsened in 2020." World Meteorological Organization, 20 Apr. 2021, public.wmo.int/en/media/press-release/climate-change-in-dicators-and-impacts-worsened-2020.

Published by Ian Tiseo, and Jun 7. "UK: Plastic Products CO2 Emissions 1990-2019." Statista, 7 June 2021, www.statista.com/statistics/485966/co2-emissions-from-the-manufacture-of-plastic-products-uk/.

Baker, Cambry, et al. "Educating for Resilience: Parent and Teacher Perceptions of Children's Emotional Needs in Response to Climate Change." Environmental Education Research, vol. 27, no. 5, 2020, pp. 687–705., doi:10.1080/135 04622.2020.1828288.

Iea. "The Carbon Footprint of Streaming Video: Fact-Checking the Headlines – Analysis." IEA, www.iea.org/ commentaries/the-carbon-footprint-of-streaming-video-fact-checking-the-headlines.

EPA, Environmental Protection Agency, www.epa.gov/gh-gemissions/sources-greenhouse-gas-emissions.

Miranda, J.D., et al. "Climatic Change and Rainfall PAT-TERNS: Effects On Semi-Arid Plant Communities of the Iberian Southeast." Journal of Arid Environments, vol. 75, no. 12, 2011, pp. 1302–1309., doi:10.1016/j. jaridenv.2011.04.022.

Raanan, Hagai, et al. "Three-Dimensional Structure and Cyanobacterial Activity within a Desert Biological SOIL CRUST." Environmental Microbiology, vol. 18, no. 2, 2015, pp. 372–383., doi:10.1111/1462-2920.12859.

"Our Mission." Eileenmuza.org, www.eileenmuza.org/.

"Biological Soil Crust Activity." National Parks Service, U.S. Department of the Interior, www.nps.gov/arch/learn/ kidsyouth/biologicalsoilcrust.htm.

TECHNICAL Note - USDA. www.nrcs.usda.gov/Internet/ FSE_PLANTMATERIALS/publications/idpmctn7064.pdf.

Flagel, David G., et al. "Fear and Loathing in a Great Lakes FOREST: Cascading Effects of Competition between Wolves and Coyotes." Journal of Mammalogy, 2016, doi:10.1093/ jmammal/gyw162.

Meachen, Julie A., et al. "Ecological Changes in Coyotes (*Canis latrans*) in Response to the Ice Age Megafaunal Extinctions." PLoS ONE, vol. 9, no. 12, 2014, doi:10.1371/ journal.pone.0116041.

Weaver. Diameter-Weight Relationships for Juniper from Wet and Dry ... www.jstor.org/stable/41711861.

Cupressaceae (Cypress FAMILY) Description, www.conifers.org/cu/Cupressaceae.php.

"Cupressaceae." Wikipedia, Wikimedia Foundation, 29 Mar. 2021, en.wikipedia.org/wiki/Cupressaceae.

"Carbon Sequestration in Different WETLAND Plant Communities in the Big Cypress Swamp Region of Southwest Florida." Taylor & Francis, www.tandfonline.com/doi/full/10.1080/21513732.2014.973909.

Christensen, Nedra K; Sorenson, ANN W; Hendricks, Deloy G; Munger, Ronald (1998). "Juniper Ash as a Source of Calcium in the Navajo Diet". Journal of the American Dietetic Association. 98 (3): 333–4. doi:10.1016/s0002-8223(98)00077-7. PMID 9508018.

Ballew, Carol; White, Linda L.; Strauss, Karen F.; Benson, Lois J.; Mendlein, James M.; Mokdad, Ali H. (1997-10-01). "Intake of Nutrients and Food Sources of Nutrients among the Navajo: Findings from the Navajo Health and Nutrition Survey". The Journal of Nutrition. 127 (10): 2085S–2093S. doi:10.1093/jn/127.10.2085s.

Leonhardt, Megan. "Older Millennials Have Lived through 2 Economic Crises-and It's Affecting Their Decisions around Having Kids." CNBC, CNBC, 18 May 2021, www.cnbc.com/2021/05/18/older-millennials-delayed-families-but-the-pandemic-made-kids-more-uncertain.html#:~:text=About%2019%25%20of%20older%20millennials,according%20to%20the%20Harris%20survey.&text=By%2040%2C%20the%20age%20the,of%20getting%20pregnant%20each%20month.

"The Indomitable Juniper." National Parks Service, U.S. Department of the Interior, www.nps.gov/cany/learn/nature/utahjuniper.htm.

Massachusetts Institute of Technology. "Carbon Footprint

Of Best Conserving Americans Is Still Double Global Average." ScienceDaily. ScienceDaily, 29 April 2008. <www.sciencedaily.com/releases/2008/04/080428120658.htm>.

"What Is Your Carbon Footprint?" The Nature Conservancy, www.nature.org/en-us/get-involved/how-to-help/carbon-footprint-calculator/#:~:text=The%20average%20carbon%20footprint%20for,under%202%20tons%20by%202050.

Nace, Trevor. "Best Way to Fight Climate Change? Clone 3,000-Year-Old Redwoods." Forbes, Forbes Magazine, 30 July 2019, www.forbes.com/sites/trevornace/2019/07/29/best-way-to-fight-climate-change-clone-3000-year-old-redwoods/?sh=168482a63c33.

Figures 1-3, collected

Doeliing, Helimut H, et al. "GEOLOGIC MAP OF THE MOAB 7.5' QUADRANGLE 7 GRAND COUNTY, UTAH ." State Contract 95-0846 STATEMAP Agreement No. 1434-94A-1256 , 26 Jan. 2002, pp. 1–38., doi:1-55791-580-6 .

Urban coyotes are genetically distinct from coyotes in natural habitats

Anthony Adducci, II, Jeremy Jasperse, Seth Riley, Justin Brown, Rodney Honeycutt, Javier Monzón

Journal of Urban Ecology, Volume 6, Issue 1, 2020, juaa010, https://doi.org/10.1093/jue/juaa010
Published: 04 May 2020 Article history

"Thriving under our noses, stealthily: coyotes" URL accessed on January 9, 2006.

Jackson, Mark. "Coyote Diet." Feeding Nature, 11 Dec. 2020, feedingnature.com/what-do-coyotes-eat/.

"Newspaper Rock". Markers and Monuments Database. Utah Department of Heritage and Arts. Archived from the original on 2013-04-03.

"Bulows, Ernest. "Navajo Taboos for Nature, Domestic and Wild Animals", Traditional Navajo Taboos". Archived from the original on 2018-12-26.

Bradshaw, John W. "The Evolutionary Basis for the Feeding Behavior of Domestic Dogs (Canis FAMILIARIS) and Cats (Felis Catus)." The Journal of Nutrition, vol. 136, no. 7, 2006, doi:10.1093/jn/136.7.1927s.

Benson, John F., et al. "Ungulate Predation and Ecological Roles of Wolves and Coyotes in Eastern North America." Ecological Applications, vol. 27, no. 3, 2017, pp. 718–733., doi:10.1002/eap.1499.

Johnson, Norman. "Faculty Opinions Recommendation of Genomic Analyses Reveal the Influence of Geographic Origin, Migration, and Hybridization on Modern Dog Breed Development." Faculty Opinions – Post-Publication Peer Review of the Biomedical Literature, 2017, doi:10.3410/f.727547314.793538816.

Melaniepoliquin, /. "Coyote (*Canis latrans*) – Ecological Profile – Section 63." Human & Wildlife Ecology, 12 Apr. 2018, humanwildlifeecology.wordpress.com/2018/02/14/coyote-canis-latrans-ecological-profile-section-63/.

Harrison, D. J. (1992, January). Dispersal Characteristics of Juvenile Coyotes in Maine. Retrieved from http://www.jstor.org/stable/3808800

Miklósi, Adam (4 December 2008). Dog Behaviour, Evolution, and Cognition. Oxford University Press. p. 205. ISBN 9780191580130.

Thanks for reading. <3 you. -Cedar

www.ingramcontent.com/pod-product-compliance
Lightning Source LLC
Chambersburg PA
CBHW022053020426
42335CB00012B/666